LONDON

NIGHT AND DAY

LONDON
NIGHT AND DAY

illustrated by

OSBERT LANCASTER

a guide to where the other books don't take you

EDITED BY SAM LAMBERT

Published in Great Britain in 2014 by Old House books & maps
c/o Osprey Publishing, PO Box 883, Oxford OX2 9PH, UK.
c/o Osprey Publishing, PO Box 3985, New York, NY 10185-3985, USA.
Website: www.oldhousebooks.co.uk

A CIP catalogue record for this book is available from the British Library.

ISBN-13: 978 1 90840 293 6

Originally published in 1951 by The Architectural Press London.
Printed in China through Worldprint Ltd.

14 15 16 17 18   10 9 8 7 6 5 4 3 2 1

CONTENTS

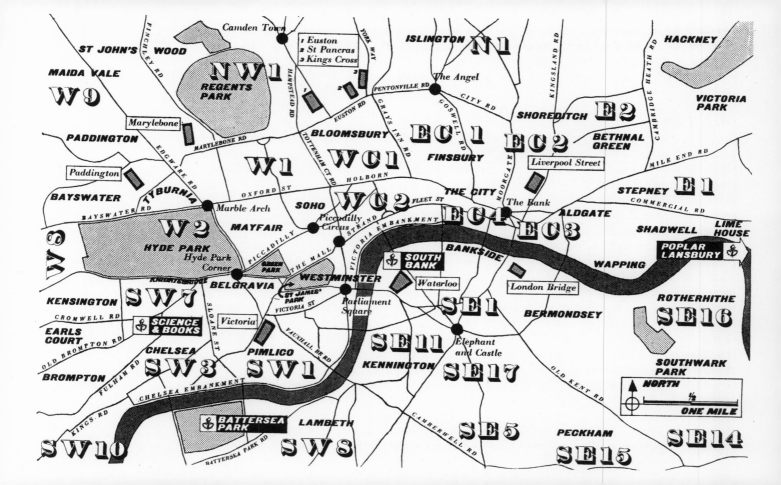

Mrs Gould and Mr Douglas and I went in the Colonel's chariot to the Haymarket. As we drove along and spoke good English, I was full of rich imagination of London, ideas suggested by the Spectator and such as I could not explain to most people, but which I strongly feel and am ravished with. My blood glows and my mind is agitated with felicity. Boswell's London Journal, 8 January 1763 *(Heinemann, 21s.)*

LONDON

Unless you are a professional Bohemian, no capital city is cheap to stay in. London is not an exception, and if you are going places, you won't do it on air. Therefore in this guide we do not concentrate on what things would cost though we mention cost where we can; you will probably decide anyway that things cost plenty. We concentrate not on what London can get out of you but on what you can get out of London. Remembering that despite austerity and war, London is still the greatest market there is anywhere for goods of a quality and craftsmanship that the world wants and can't otherwise get.

Let us warn you right at the start, London is a misleading city. Except to the trained romantic its surface appearances are banal ; and unlike Paris, whose charms are discernible when first you drive along the main thoroughfares, its main thoroughfares are far the most hideous part of it. Its charms are hidden round the corner and only to be enjoyed by those who seek them out. One purpose of this guide is to help those who seek them out to find them. *Above* the surface, with its incorruptible police and oh-so-practical local authorities, who care so much about the letter—drains and fire protection—and so little about the spirit of the law, London is a machine for doing business in, for getting workers to work in.

Beneath the surface London is the world's greatest man-hive, not merely in numbers of citizens (a meaningless criterion) but in variety of action—the Athens, New York, Washington, Monte Carlo, Singapore, Hollywood, Forest Hills, Ancient Rome of about a quarter of the Earth's inhabitants. Thus if you walk down Bond Street it is a good bet that you will be, at sometime or other, within a few yards of an international crook, a *ditto* financier, a literary genius, a sea-captain, a King, a *femme fatale*, a famous athlete, a Royal couturier, a Scottish

MAPS

Alas, there's room in this guide for only one small map, so characted as to give you a general idea (we're sorry it's no more) where the street you want to find is. Reference is from the postal area given in the address, to the postal area shown on the map (W.C.1, E.C.15, etc.). The rest of the work you'll have to do yourself from other maps or helpful policemen. We're sorry about this, but to give a really efficient map service for the sort of out-of-the-way things we direct you to, would require another book of maps the size of this, an unnecessary duplication, since good ones exist already. What we have done is to suggest maps and where to get them under the *Maps and Guidebooks* heading of SHOPPING (9 a.m.).

laird, an English duchess, a great painter, an empire builder, a spy, a sultan, a field-marshal or a legislator. London is the world's greatest get-together, not so much of types, classes, races, as of individual departures from the norm. And if you take the trouble to peer beyond the fronts of the great shopping streets into the almost secret places behind—the Georgian alleys, the intimate pubs, the little markets, the masked mews, the squares filled with great trees, the hidden " yards " covered in cobbles ; or, better still, penetrate into the cosy clubs, grand salons, panelled chambers, bar parlours, that lie behind these façades, you will begin to discover the London that hypnotised Boswell and Dickens. A London that built and backed the Commonwealth; a London of significant individuals leading a vast variety of individual lives, in a vast variety of individual ways, heroic and unheroic, major and minor, savoury and unsavoury, legal and illegal—yet achieving despite that individualism a certain community, even strength, of purpose. And still, despite blitzes and convulsions, strong in its original virtue of non-conformity.

The 20th century, in trying to conveyor-belt us all, has made a big effort to standardise London. But the essential London is only half standardised, and may beat the conveyor-belt yet. If you have eyes to see and a soul to love it, that other unstandardised half is still there for the finding. Our job in this guide is to help you, the visitor, to find it. Forgive us if we credit you with ignorance you are far from having. Obviously we have to write for those who don't know the answers. Obviously, on the other hand, there is a limit in terms of grape-vine to what the printed, as opposed to the whispered, word can achieve. Within these limitations we try, in what follows, to break through the surface generalisations of the standardised guide books to that living tissue of skills, specialisations, appetites, graces, eccentricities and solicitudes, that have made London the place it is, so that you in your turn, dear visitor, may learn how to break into a ducal home, a murder trial, Savile Row, a theatre-club, the House of Commons, a night-club. So that you may know at last where to get the best glass eye, riding boots, moussaka, glimpse of the 18th century, riverside pub, jazz, coffee ; even so that you may know where to pawn your watch. Our motto for the visitor to London is—look beneath the surface. And in the pages which follow Osbert Lancaster, the doyen of London nonconformity, supports our stream of good advice with drawings that eloquently evoke London's other under-surface look.

7 am

HOW IT BEGAN

First thing to understand clearly is that where there are no roads, rivers act as highways. Always have, always will. Hence in pre-Roman days the big river so close to the mainland of Europe (swampy and forested but with gravel patches, useful sites for bridges or fords), became the natural entry into Britain for all the adventurers who were out to exploit this little-known island, mild of climate, fertile of soil, and good for oysters, pearls, hunting dogs, tin and gold.

first Londoners

Whatever settlements might be started on the river bank, the spot that would eventually come out on top would be the lowest place on the river capable of carrying a bridge. The bridge builders would look for a narrowing of the banks, a gravel bed for the foundations and a hill to build their settlement upon, out of reach of floods. The site was found, a bridge was built, and under the Romans, if not before, London started its great adventure as a port, bridge, and bridge head settlement, controlling communications between north and south Britain. The south bank was marshy but the north had two good hills. So the Romans, who were practical men, built on the north bank, on one hill (reputedly), a forum and basilica and on the other, a temple: two institutions which dominated the plan of London for two thousand years and are perpetuated still in St. Paul's (the temple) and Leadenhall Market (the forum). In the valley between them ran a river (The Walbrook), which still runs out under Cannon Street Station. Another river (The Fleet) protected the west flank of the city—if you are interested you can see it still by looking down the manholes in Farringdon Street.

London growing

Once this simple fact of history is understood the plan of London, otherwise quite incomprehensible, becomes almost easy. On the map you will see all the main arteries radiate from, or find their way to, the bridgehead settlement at London Bridge. The Roman town, in fact, surrounded by its wall (London Wall), perpetuated to-day in what is known all the world over as the " City."

the second city
In course of time London Wall found itself unable to contain all the citizens, and now the Thames, acting as a kind of linear magnet, began to draw off pieces towards the head piece, the King, who had set up his court at Westminster (the nearest ford). Thus a new focus of interest and magnet of population was started in competition with the City, a very strong one too, since it included also a big ecclesiastical centre, Westminster Abbey. But the Palace and Westminster Abbey were bogged down amongst the marshes and in the end the swelling population of nobles and their retainers were forced away to the higher ground just north of what is now St. James's Park. First north of the Strand (Covent Garden and Lincoln's Inn), then westwards to Piccadilly (the West End and Mayfair), westwards (in Victorian times) to Belgravia, westwards to Kensington. At the other, the east end of the city, the Thames—exercising the same magnetic attraction, but for business rather than pleasure—drew off large populations of workers to its victualling yards and docks.

villages of London
The rest of the story is the old one of the Great Wen (as Cobbett called it) absorbing its surrounding villages—Marylebone (Marylebone Lane, running from Oxford Street north to Marylebone High Street, is worth following just to see what happens to a country lane that is submerged by London), Chelsea, Paddington, to the west; Hackney and Bow to the north; to the south across the river (where Bankside had already become infamous for bear-baiting, harlotry

and Shakespeare), Camberwell, Dulwich, Greenwich, Battersea, Streatham and so on. To-day there are hundreds more. You have to imagine the influential people taking up residence, first in what they fondly regarded as suburban retreats, then the spaces in between being filled in with a lava-flow of " working classes." To-day London has no visible pattern, except that which is the result of the initial tensions set up between the Roman bridgehead and the river front. No pattern, no plan, no high street—except the Thames, once crowded, now for a hundred years (until the water-buses) as good as closed and boarded up.

8 am
LET ME OUT

Rather odd to bustle you out of London hardly before you get in? We aren't really doing that. It happens that when you do decide to make a day of it in the (London) country you *will* have to make a day of it—which means early decisions. Here is the tactful breakfast-table reminder. Up river to Richmond? Down river to Greenwich? Or all the way to see some local country house? Whichever way, boats or cars are at your service,

punts putting out their awnings, waiters their tables, the river its white sails and red.

down Thames

A map of London shows one thing clearly; London has no High Street. The Thames has no name-plate, but High Street it was until about 1820. Remember that and the things said under 7 a.m. and the Plan of London begins to make sense. That year over 3,000 wherries plied the river. The call was " Oars " (not " Taxi ") at the top of any of the 17 public stairs between Lambeth and Limehouse. But in 1829 came the omnibus and in 1836 the railway, and the river lost favour with travellers. In 1905 the L.C.C. put 30 paddle steamers on the river hoping to revive the river's popularity, but the experiment (odd word) was a flop. The steamers ended up at places as far apart as Loch Lomond and the River Tigris. In 1940 a service between Westminster and Woolwich, taking two hours, ran two months only—people preferred tram, which took half as long. Now there has been another revolution in taste, and since 1948 the new water-buses have been a glorious success. If to-day is fine try one for your first look at London—only don't choose the rush hours. Embark (if you are in the West End) at Westminster Pier (in Big Ben's shadow, and in charge of piermaster Harding), or, if at the South Bank, from Rodney Pier (Dome of Discovery) or Nelson Pier (Royal Festival Hall). Landlubbers and visitors will not know that there are six new piers on the river this year, these two and you will be calling at two more, Blackfriars and Old Swan. Or, if you're the independent type, ring up Alec Metcalf (ELT. 1627) who will provide you with motor boat and man at 30s. an hour. Boat holds twelve so if your harem is with you it will work out quite cheap. Greenwich would cost about a fiver. The river is divided into three sections for administration purposes. The Upper section from Teddington Lock to the Tower, the Middle section down to Erith and the Lower section down to the Nore. The harbour master is Commander Coleman, and you might see him in his launch M/L "Nore," anywhere. Under him will be three assistant harbour masters: Captain Lovell in the Upper section in his launch "Ranelagh;" Captain Letts," Ravensbourne," in the Middle section and the "Ray" and "Roding" are other duty launches in this section. Just one of the harbour master's jobs might be to see that barges are not tied up more than three deep alongside any one ship. Two other ways to Greenwich we recommend (one detailed later), by London's oldest railway line and on foot. Both interesting and the railway (built 1836) takes you to London Bridge. You can of course go right down to Margate and Ramsgate, or right up to Oxford (with changes) by some of the bigger steamers from Westminster pier.

STARTING DOWNSTREAM, first item immediately to starboard is the South Bank Exhibition, once a warehouse area, originally site of marshy and thickly wooded Paris gardens used as a bear and bull baiting ground in Elizabeth's day. Shot tower used since 1789 for making shot for England's wars is now a radio telescope and lighthouse at the South Bank (its interior is an architectural experience, so don't miss going inside when you visit the Festival).

HUNGERFORD BRIDGE. Until 85 years ago a road suspension bridge. Dismantled, parts were used in the construction of the Clifton Suspension Bridge. But you can still see the two main supports of the old bridge. Both were in the river once, but the one to port is now incorporated in the Victoria Embankment. LOOK OUT FOR orange lights over certain arches of bridges—indicate navigable channel.

PORT, YORK GATE AND WATERSTAIRS (by Inigo Jones), one time back door on the Thames for York House (designed by Inigo for George Villiers, first Duke of Buckingham). Interesting because it shows you position of river bank in Pepys' day.

WATERLOO BRIDGE

PORT, END OF THE VICTORIA EMBANKMENT. Try to spot a 5 ft. model lighthouse, a simple concrete affair cast round a pipe

(we could have made it). Reputedly the work of a pilot named Taylor (c. 1910) and until the blitz, on the other side of the river.

BLACKFRIARS BRIDGE. Port, underneath the bridge, the onetime exit of the Fleet river, next most historic London stream to Thames, could be seen at low tide. Runs through sewers now.

PORT, QUEENHITHE (you will recognise it as a little harbour). In the time of Henry II this wharf and that at Billingsgate were the only permitted berthing places for ships. As you draw abreast LOOK OUT FOR a glimpse of St. Paul's between the warehouses.

LOOK OUT FOR foreshoremen (nick-named mudlarks) now that you are in the warehouse area, whose job it is to push mud on the banks back into the river at low tide, so that barges (left high and dry at low tide) won't slide off.

LOOK OUT FOR a barge under oar. (Becoming rare these days.) Such a barge (just as an L car is in charge of a qualified driver) will be in charge of a Freeman of the Company of Watermen and Lightermen of the River Thames. With the Freeman may be (apart from another Freeman, of course) an apprentice. It takes five years to become a Freeman. He is also allowed to pilot small vessels (such as the river steamer you are now on), a skiff, collier or barge. Apprentices have to appear at the Court of Binding (at the time of being bound), whereupon they become Unlicensed Boys, and again after two years, when they become Licensed Apprentices and again after five years, at least, to qualify for their freedom.

SOUTHWARK BRIDGE. First bridge built here 1819.

LOOK OUT FOR RIVERSIDE PUBS. You will pass six in all. These you probably would not be able to recognise were it not for the large brewery notices. You are passing the first one now, to starboard, BARCLAY, the "Anchor," Bankside; you may just have been told that you have seen the site of the Globe Theatre. We're sorry, but according to the best authority this is not so. The Shakespeare Reading Society has erected a bronze plaque on the brewery wall in Park Street, which is near enough to the correct site—but not on the river. There's one more myth we have to explode while you're passing Bankside. There is no evidence to show that Wren lived in any existing house on Bankside, while St. Paul's was being built. The oldest house left is No. 49, which was built in 1712 (St. Paul's was completed 1710).

STARBOARD, BANKSIDE, almost as famous as Strand. Since Shakespearian times, London's Bohemia, filled with playhouses, tarts, pimps, bear-baiting rings, spivs, authors and taverns. Nothing left now but warehouses—and the Anchor.

LONDON BRIDGE. Built and rebuilt many times. The last time in 1831 to replace the famous bridge (but positioned upstream) which, because of its enormous piers, would have made your passage through its arches (smooth enough now) like shooting the rapids (most people preferred to climb ashore and take another boat the other side). In winter piers sometimes got blocked with ice and then river froze over above London Bridge—hence the ice fairs celebrated in song, story and picture.

POOL OF LONDON, you are now in it. Take a good look because it happens to be the most celebrated pocket handkerchief of water in the world. Not very impressed? Don't worry, it'll grow on you. To port St. Paul's, the Tower and the City, with all it means in terms of association; to starboard a forest of cranes, a Venetian canal-scape of warehouses. The Pool is the water between London Bridge and Tower Bridge but all down the river now you will see the drama of the world's greatest port blitzed and unblitzed, with the great ships all round. There are really only two people employed in mooring ships (carrying hawsers from ship to shore, etc.). They are Mr. Metcalf and Mr. Smith. Look out for their motor boats.

PORT, ADELAIDE HOUSE. Belongs to London City Buildings. On the eighth floor is a roof garden. So next time you're that way pay a call because the garden is public. Just go in at the entrance in King William Street, take a lift to the seventh floor. Walk up a flight of stairs and there you are. No seats, BUT a miniature golf course, and, of course, flowers. Popular place for city workers with sandwich lunches. Open 9.0 to 5.30. Before the war they used to keep bees up there and during the war they grew potatoes.

PORT, MONUMENT, once on one side of London Bridge approach.

PORT, ST. MAGNUS THE MARTYR. Once abutting *Old* London Bridge (new bridge upstream). Paving stones from the old bridge can be seen at base of the steeple, through which

"city workers," coming from Camberwell or Kennington, used to pass.

PORT, BILLINGSGATE (full description of fishy smells at 5 a.m.).

PORT, H.M.S. HARPY (as you can see it's no ship). It's the pier where H.M. Customs and Excise launches tie up. Behind it, Custom House.

PORT, A PADDLE STEAMER. Hardly recognisable shorn of its paddles, well over 40 years old and once on the Gosport ferry service. One time houseboat belonging (so we are told) to Lady Astor, now owned by sea scouts, who will be pleased to show you round Saturday afternoons or Sundays.

PORT, TOWER OF LONDON, built by William the Conqueror just outside London Wall to control (and threaten) city. Garrisoned by Yeomen Warders (" Beefeaters ") in 15th century costume, 37 of them on duty by day. White Tower (Portland stone) contains armouries and the oldest museum in England. Beauchamp Tower and Salt Tower used for respectable and not so respectable prisoners respectively, and Wakefield Tower, the Crown Jewels. A fine distinction: Tower Green was used for private executions and Tower Hill for public ones. King's menagerie kept here until 1834. Ravens which still haunt the Tower may be remains of it. Best thing, chapel of St. John, tiny but sublime, massive early Norman.

PORT, TOWER PIER. At Tower Wharf, which follows, LOOK OUT FOR the walled-up entrance to the Traitor's Gate. At low tide the beach below (artificial freak, a strip of pure sand) acts as *plage* for all the small boys in the city—river wall of Tower (public) excellent place for sandwich luncheon on hot day. If the seats are full sit on the cannon. For light relief there will probably be a row going on on Tower Hill, which, like Marble Arch, is a traditional haunt of public orators.

TOWER BRIDGE (Scottish Baronial style, opened in 1894), last bridge before the sea. The 1,200-ton bascules take 1½ minutes to rise and are operated three or four times a day. A staff of eighty works the bridge. We are sorry but you cannot see the working of the mechanism, nor cross by the 141 ft. high footway.

PORT, COLONIAL WHARVES. You will probably see a French steamer, of the type that goes up the Seine, berthed here, probably the

" Dijonnais." She comes over once a fortnight.

LOOK OUT FOR FOREIGN SHIPS. Irrespective of nationality they fly the red ensign from the foremast when in a British port.

STARBOARD, CHERRY GARDEN PIER, site of public garden in Pepys' day. Alight here for " Angel " and " Torbay " Inns (see 6 p.m.). Along this bank are a few of the public stairs leading to the water's edge, with names such as Rotherhithe, King's, Prince's, Elephant, Globe, Horseferry, Pageant, Cuckold's Point, Acorn and Dog and Duck. Most of them still rights of way, but locked to prevent children falling into the water.

PORT, WAPPING NEW STAIRS and Wapping Old Stairs (blocked off), mentioned by Dibden in a song. Sailors coming ashore here in the old days were often robbed by women who made their living this way.

STARBOARD, THE SIGN OF COURAGE, " Angel," Rotherhithe.

STARBOARD, THE SIGN OF MEUX, " Torbay," Rotherhithe.

STARBOARD, THE SIGN OF CHARRINGTON, " Spread Eagle."

PORT AND STARBOARD. The circular, white stone and red brick ventilation shafts of the Rotherhithe tunnel.

STARBOARD, LAVENDER WHARF. W. B. Dick & Co., Ltd. In fog pilots smell their way up river. Well, this is one of the places they smell. And the distinctive smell is that produced in the processing of mineral lubricating oils. You may get a whiff of it, too.

STARBOARD, ALONG THE RIVER, near and round about Rotherhithe is a man who makes his living by (shooting and) selling pigeons. You can always tell grain barges by the presence of these pigeons, which, of course, in this case are considered pests (probably an entirely different tribe from those resident in Trafalgar Square, so a great amount of sympathy is not necessary).

PORT, THE SIGN OF MANN AND CROSSMAN, " Prospect of Whitby," Wapping.

PORT, THE SIGN OF TAYLOR WALKER, " Grapes," Limehouse.

STARBOARD, THE OLD SMALLPOX PIER (where those with the malady were landed). Now just a river fire station.

STARBOARD, COMMERCIAL DOCK entrance, leading to Greenland Dock, once centre for the Greenland whale fisheries, previously called Howland Dock and site of London's first dock.

STARBOARD, ROYAL VICTORIA VICTUALLING YARD, 35 acres, largest of the three Naval victualling yards before the war.

LOOK OUT FOR, when passing the various entrances to docks, the flags that fly. A red one indicates that a ship is coming out of the dock. A blue one is the all-clear signal for incoming ships.

on foot, for bad sailors

Start your walk at the Tower. Follow river along Tower Gardens under Tower Bridge into St. Katharine's Way, which becomes Wapping High Street. A highly melodramatic change from the rustic to the industrial. At the end of it is the 'Prospect of Whitby' (a good place for a pint and a look at the river from the balcony at the ground floor back). Continue along Garnet Street, right into Wapping Wall, which becomes Glamis Road, and then into The Highway. This route will take you through an area of cobbled roadways, tall warehouses, linked across the road by metal bridges, and studded with cranes, corner pubs— battened up—bridges over the entrances to the various docks, some used no longer. A tremendous combination of Doré and Piranesi, interspersed with pre-Victorian relics, of the old village network, like the church of St. John, Wapping, and the quayside buildings alongside the swing bridge. Linger here if you want to reconstruct Cruikshank's London, and don't miss the sinister wall of St. Katharine's Dock. From the Highway into Narrow Street. Follow Narrow Street eastwards along river for $\frac{1}{2}$ m. through once romantic Chinatown of Limehouse. Right down Emmett Street to West Ferry Road. From here take a bus which runs along western side of Isle of Dogs (apparently so called by seamen hearing cry of hounds kennelled in area over which Kings staying at Greenwich Palace hunted) to the terminus at Ferry Street. Upper deck view of river to right and West India Docks to left. At bus terminus, turn towards river. Good view across river of Royal Naval College, from small green open space, Island Gardens. Here also entrance to tunnel (foot passengers

only) under Thames to *Greenwich*. Tunnel emerges in Greenwich Church Street in old Greenwich. (*Greenwich Hospital* alongside can either be inspected now or on way back as described later). Along river to N.W. is Deptford, of shipbuilding and Royal Victualling yard fame ; to E. lies Woolwich (Royal Arsenal and one time home of ' the Shop ').

St. Alphage Church (rebuilt 1718), bomb-damaged, in Greenwich Church Street, contains tombs of Thomas Tallis (cathedral music), General Wolfe and first ' Polly Peachum ' (Lavinia Fen-

ton). Henry VIII baptised there. Follow Greenwich Church Street to junction with Greenwich High Road. Then take second turning on left, Royal Hill. Again take second on left, Gloucester Circus, leading into Croom's Hill—little oasis of unspoilt Georgian houses.

At top of Croom's Hill on left is *Greenwich Park* (laid out by Louis XIV's Le Notre in 17th century). Enter park at park entrance and proceed eastwards until reaching Blackheath Avenue. Turn left and follow Blackheath Avenue to building of

Royal Observatory, founded 1675 (*Octagon Room* by Wren). Greenwich meridian passes through it. (But Royal Observatory organisation was recently moved to Hurstmonceux Castle in Sussex, to escape London's climate). From here one of very best views of London.

See, if possible : about ¼ mile E. *Magnetic Pavilion* close to remains of Roman Villa discovered 1902. In S.W. corner of park the *Ranger's House* bought 1753 by E. of Chesterfield (' Letters to my Son ') and once owned by Lord Wolseley ; also *Macartney House*, home of another soldier's, Wolfe's, parents. On E. side, in Maze Hill, *Vanbrugh Castle* built by Vanbrugh 1714.

Now two possibilities. Either descend hill to explore Greenwich Hospital or, preferably, retrace steps along Blackheath Avenue out of park and proceed across *Blackheath* (famous for Dover Road highwaymen, as rendezvous of rebels Wat Tyler and Jack Cade, and for first golf course built in England in 1608, but not now used). *Blackheath Village*, beyond, another left-over of 18th century, highly notable for elegance of *Royal Parade*, *Montpelier Row*, *Tranquil Vale* and *The Paragon*. *Morden College* (almshouses), behind The Paragon, fine Wren example.

up Thames

Going up river is even more rewarding than going down. Ships with large funnels, larger bars, will get you up to Windsor, Eton, Henley, Oxford (the last, not on the same day), but these are out of our beat. Best thing, we think, is to get you on the tow-path, which means you will be able to stop and enjoy quayside and 18th-century riverside-village life. Here London shows its most intimate face, and in the walks that follow we try to work in the major delights. Start from Hammersmith Bridge, prepare for red Georgian houses, large trees, cobbled quays, hards. Prepare also for strange

industrial monstrosities and some suburban ones too. It is the mixture of these which gives the scene its poignancy.

first walk, Hammersmith to Kew (approx. 4 m.)

From Putney (only 6 miles from Hyde Park Corner) the Thames towpath follows the river to its source at Cricklade 150 miles upstream. Only difficulty is where it jumps from one bank of river to the other, necessitating a ferry which isn't always there. Take a walk along part of this path, through Chiswick, and you won't regret it. Best place to start, Hammersmith Bridge. (Underground to HAMMERSMITH BROADWAY District and Piccadilly lines —leaving station, turn left down HAMMERSMITH BRIDGE ROAD— or bus 73 to Hammersmith Bridge.) Just before bridge turn right on to LOWER MALL (tow-path here is other side, but this north bank is more interesting). Here are Rowing Club and (very special) DOVES INN, with tables to drink in garden overlooking the river ; former house of Doves Press (Cobden-Sanderson) on right. Lower Mall leads to UPPER MALL and terrace of

Georgian houses with gardens to river (KELMSCOTT HOUSE, home of William Morris, 1878 to 1896—in 1816 Sir Francis Ronalds laid first electric cable in its gardens). Just beyond, notice junction of GRAND UNION CANAL with Thames. Turn right here, down EYOT GARDENS, to look at ST. PETER'S SQUARE (Regency), then retrace steps riverwards to Black Lion pub (see 6 p.m.), HAMMERSMITH TERRACE and CHISWICK MALL with WALPOLE HOUSE (reputedly Thackeray's prep. school, brought into VANITY FAIR and perhaps the nicest Georgian house in London). On Chiswick Mall the Thames bank reverts to grass for first time since leaving London. At the end is a genuine Hard, with boats and a possible ferry, and then CHURCH STREET and ST. NICHOLAS CHURCH (Hogarth, Kent buried there). Church Street still typical village street. Satisfying Georgian houses in CHISWICK SQUARE and Hogarth's house in HOGARTH LANE. Turn left to nearest entrance to CHISWICK PARK, formerly grounds of Palladian CHISWICK HOUSE, built by Kent about 1730 for Lord Burlington. Fox had his last illness here in 1806, and Canning died here, 1827. Leave park by southern entrance into BURLINGTON LANE, then after dull half-mile, cross railway at SUTTON LANE ROAD, and then follow GROVE PARK ROAD, until this road reaches river at STRAND-ON-THE-GREEN, much rebuilt but still pleasant relic of 18th-century London. Half mile of river flanked by continuous Georgian houses. Only blot on landscape—the railway bridge. Pubs : THE BULL'S HEAD (for snacks) and THE CITY BARGE. (Alternatively, meals procurable at restaurants further on at Kew). Continue to KEW BRIDGE. Cross river to KEW GREEN, divinely Georgian and perfect setting for the cricket match you may find going on if it is a Saturday. St. Anne's Church, 1714, is where Gainsborough (1788) and Zoffany (1810) are buried. Facing Green are gates of KEW GARDENS (the Royal Botanical Gardens), containing 25,000 varieties of plants. Once the grounds of Kew Palace, the Gardens were mostly originated by Princess Augusta, mother of George III, in 1759; Sir William Chambers added follies and temples (see his PAGODA) when it was fashionable to go Chinese. The Brazilian rubber plants which established the rubber industry in Malaya and Ceylon were raised here. Look out for insect-eating plants in the Succulent House. Good guide book explains what to see in way of flowering plants at each time of year.

second walk, Kew to Hampton Court (approx. 5 m. on foot)
This walk starts at point where walk No. 1 finished. Leave Kew Gardens by gates to Kew Palace. Turn left along towpath on Surrey side, one of best stretches of river anywhere; on left Kew Gardens, on right, across river, Syon Park. After 1½ miles, cross by ferry to ISLEWORTH to make diversion to Syon House and Brentford beyond. Land at quay (opposite THE LONDON APPRENTICE). Turn right and, after 50 yards, enter iron gates of footpath to home of Dukes of Northumberland. Legend says footpath is public because Henry VIII's body was carried along it to Syon on funeral route from Westminster to Windsor (ground over which king's body travels remains public thereafter). Syon House, unique ducal oasis left over from past age is usually open in summer, Weds., Thurs., Fris., and Sats. Present splendour dates from mid-eighteenth century when Sir Hugh Smithson (D. of Northumberland) gave Robert Adam unlimited scope. Leaving, continue along footpath to LONDON ROAD (Roman Road) on North side of park. To right BRENTFORD HIGH STREET (where R. Brent joins Thames) retains slight appearance of town in Bath hey-day. Turn left along London Road, passing Adam's entrance gates to Syon and his SCREEN and, nearly opposite, neglected Georgian house with dilapidated gazebo above garden wall (once Dr. Medwin's Academy—preparatory school of Shelley, John Rennie and others).

Turn left down PARK ROAD and return to river side at ISLEWORTH (where Van Gogh once lived). Take a drink at the ancient (and delightful and very Georgian) LONDON APPRENTICE (with plaster decorations on dining room ceiling probably by Italian craftsmen working at Syon House) situated on one of London's very nicest quays which has been from medieval times a free dock presented by Syon nuns. Craft still tie up for four tides free of charge. Quay looks across river to OLD DEER PARK of Richmond Palace and ROYAL MID-SURREY G.C. On wall of bombed church alongside (by Wren) sun-dial tells time in London, Jamaica, Moscow and Jerusalem simultaneously (locals will probably say it was put up by a sailor with wife in each port). Good houses in THE SQUARE further on, and further on still at 158 TWICKENHAM ROAD, is house where Van Gogh lived during his strange English adventure. From Square walk 1 mile to Richmond Bridge (via RICHMOND ROAD, left along RAILSHEAD ROAD, across TWICKENHAM BRIDGE, along towpath) and take steamer to HAMPTON COURT PALACE.

After you've done the Palace and the maze we reckon it will be dinner time and you may be too exhausted to get back to London. If so there are some excellent alternatives. One is to dine at the very slap-up Mitre opposite the gates, or the Kings Arms Hotel. Another (if you have the strength) is to take a 15-minute walk along the towpath (downstream). If Fred Painter is not waiting to take you across to THAMES DITTON (at the steps), then shout for him (ferry fee, 3d.). Dine at the Swan (Ye Olde Swan), 13th-century, still a modest 4s.; the cusine, very English. Décor, floor on several levels, low ceiling, oak panelling, sporting prints, lighting intimate, mostly table-bound (which makes it a good place for dinner). Cutlery from the Lakeside Hotel, Windermere (bought from a friend, retired and living in Monte Carlo). Thames Ditton is one of the best examples you are likely to find of a charming old suburban village.

OTHER PEOPLE'S HOMES
Most difficult of all for the visitor to England is to get behind the

public façade of hotel-restaurant life into what are called the homes of the people. It happens that a section of " the people," and that, decoratively speaking, the most interesting, has found it expedient, because of taxation, to open their homes (for a fee) to anyone who cares to walk up the drive. So whatever else you can't get in England, there never was such a time for seeing how the nobs live, which means being allowed to peer, without any suspicion of ill-breeding, into the most closely guarded privacies of the most privileged class in Europe. A tempting thought, particularly as one can get oneself a liberal education in the fine arts at the same time. We have compiled a short list of the big houses within a thirty miles radius of London whose ducal or other owners are tremblingly eager to ask you in. Tremblingly, because big competition is developing amongst the ducal classes as to who can nobble the biggest public. Blenheim is highly fancied, but Longleat has solid backing (neither unfortun-

ately is within our thirty mile limit). If you go, don't tip the guide who takes you round—it may be the Duke—just thank him very nicely. Some of the homes we mention are of course not still lived in by the families who have owned them for generations; some are owned by the Nation or the National Trust ; all are within easy reach of London, are open to the public during some part of the year, and are, we think, well worth visiting. If our space-limited selection does not satisfy you, the National Trust, or the British Travel Association, will be able to supply you with a further list. Certain other private houses and/or gardens are opened in aid of charity from time to time. The Queen's Institute of District Nursing, 57, Lower Belgrave Street, S.W.1 (SLOane 4091) will say which and when.

CLANDON PARK. Early Georgian home of Earl of Onslow. Built in 1720 for Onslow family. One of few remaining examples of work of the Venetian, Leoni. Still substantially the same, except massive porch and terrace added, to present Earl's regret. Contains some of finest plaster work in country. Gardens by " Capability " Brown. At Guildford, Surrey, 30 miles out (train from Waterloo). Wednesday and Sunday, 2.0-6.0; Tuesday, Friday, Saturday, Bank Holidays, 11.0-6.0. Admission 2s. 6d. Connoisseurs (on alternate Thursdays) 5s.

CHARLTON HOUSE. The best surviving Jacobean country house in the County of London, now property of Greenwich Borough Council. To see over, apply to Curator. Badly blitzed at one end, see if you can notice the restoration. Good ceilings and exceptional fireplaces. Public lavatory in a corner of the grounds, in a building which for no good reason has been attributed to Inigo Jones. At Charlton, 7½ miles out (train from Charing Cross). Monday to Saturday, by arrangement with Mr. T. L. Jenkins (GREenwich 3951).

CLIVEDEN. Victorian. Built in a sumptuous Italianate style by Sir Charles Barry. Superb setting overlooking great hangers and Cliveden Reach of the Thames. Famous as home of English branch of the Astors (Lord Astor) whose week-end house parties between the wars were supposed to settle policy of

British Government—until Ribbentrop and Hitler settled it for them. Maidenhead, 24 miles out (train from Paddington). Thursdays (April-October), 2.30-5.30. No dogs.

HATCHLANDS. Medium-sized Adam house, very good ceilings, etc. Admiral Boscawen associations. The house was made over to the National Trust by Mr. H. S. Goodhart-Rendel, past president of the R.I.B.A. and brilliant writer on architecture, who still lives in it. Between Leatherhead and Guildford, Surrey, 20 miles out (train from Waterloo). Tuesday (May 3—September 30), and every Wednesday, 11.0-7.0.

HATFIELD HOUSE. Seat of Marquess of Salisbury. Originally the Old Tudor Palace, Hatfield, built by Cardinal Morton in 1497. Appropriated by Henry VIII; here he imprisoned Mary Tudor, who in turn later imprisoned Elizabeth. You can have tea in the Old (Bishop's) Palace; don't miss the Gatehouse and view down street of Hatfield from it; also first Lord Salisbury's tomb in Village Church. At Hatfield, Hertfordshire, 20 miles out (train from King's Cross ; Green Line, 716, 717, from Hyde Park Corner). Weekdays, 10.30-5.30.

HAM HOUSE. An almost perfect and little-altered seventeenth-century house, with Thames-side garden and park (walk along towpath from Richmond). Given to nation by Sir Lyonel Tollemache and now run as a museum by the Victoria and Albert. At Petersham, Surrey, 11 miles out (Green Line, 714, 716, 717 from Hyde Park Corner). Weekdays, 10.0-6.0; Sunday, 2.30-6.0.

HUGHENDEN MANOR. Individual interpretation of Gothic by E. B. Lamb. Remodelled for Benjamin Disraeli, Earl of Beaconsfield, who bought it, 1847. Interior redecoration carried out with exceptional intelligence, conjuring up the atmosphere of the period and the personality of Disraeli. At High Wycombe, Buckinghamshire, 29 miles out (train from Paddington or Marylebone, bus on from High Wycombe). Tuesday to Friday, 2.0-6.0; Saturday and Sunday, 10.0-1.0, 2.0-6.0.

KENWOOD HOUSE. Mainly Adam house. The library (now called the Adam Room) is one of the finest things Robert Adam ever did. Some fine eighteenth-century furniture and many notable pictures; Rembrandt, Gainsborough (landscape and portraits), Reynolds at his most stylish, rather too many Romneys for everyone's taste. Curiously this is the place to go to find out why Delacroix admired the young Landseer Splendid landscaped setting with lakes. Don't miss the tinker's caravan in park (summer only) beyond the stables, or the travelling coach in the latter. At Highgate (Northern Line to Hampstead or Highgate, 210 bus over the Heath). Weekdays 10.0-6.0; Sundays 2.30-6.0.

KNOLE HOUSE. Most famous Tudor house near London. Appropriated from Cranmer by Henry VIII in 1555. Given by Elizabeth to Robert Dudley, Earl of Leicester and later to Thomas Sackville (1566). It remained in the family, still there, until 1946 when it was presented to the National Trust. 365 rooms, 52 staircases, 7 courts. Look out for the Great Hall (built *c*. 1460), Ballroom, King's Bedroom with solid silver furniture and Charles I billiard table. At Sevenoaks, Kent, 24 miles out (train from Charing Cross; Green Line 704, 705 from Victoria). Open Wednesday to Saturday, 10.0-12.0 and 2.0-4.30.

LUTON HOO. Adam house, much spoiled, but containing celebrated art collection. Near Luton, Bedfordshire, 30 miles out (train from King's Cross via Hatfield), Monday, Wednesday, Thursday, Saturday, 11.0-6.0.

OSTERLEY PARK. First built in the sixteenth century. Main rebuilding done by Robert Adam for the Child family (Bankers). Look out for the Rubens painting *Apotheosis of Buckingham* at end of Gallery and another Rubens on ceiling of staircase; the pink Tapestry Room with unique Boucher-Neilson tapestries and matching furniture; the many lovely pieces of Adam furniture and the view of park from the portico. Given to National Trust in 1949 by 9th Earl of Jersey. Will be run, on similar lines to Ham House, by the Victoria and Albert Museum, who hope to open it to public some time during summer. At Isleworth, Middlesex, 12 miles out (Piccadilly Line to Osterley). For times ring Victoria and Albert Museum (KENsington 6371).

PENSHURST PLACE. Mediæval fortified manor house, first owned by Sir John de Pulteney, four times Lord Mayor of London. The Hall, complete with screens and passage, and stairs to Solar, built *c*. 1340; King's Tower added 1585 and Long Gallery 1607. Sir Philip Sidney lived here. Lord de L'Isle and Dudley is the present owner. At Penshurst, Kent, 30 miles out (train from Victoria). Try lunch at The Leicester Arms. Wednesday, Thursday, Saturday until October 13 and following

Sundays, May 13 and 27, June 10 and 24, July 8 and 22, August 5 and 19, September 2 and 16, October 7, 2.0-5.0.

POLESDEN LACEY. Edwardian-neo-Georgian country house-party atmosphere. House dull architecturally but many fine things in it. Fine gardens. Some of the best Dutch landscape paintings to be seen in England. Signed photographs, etc. (Try to see visitors' book, which is not always on view because some people never get any further). Between Bookham and Dorking, Surrey, 20 miles out (train from Waterloo). Wednesday, 2.0-6.0; Saturday, Sunday, 11.0-1.0, 2.0-6.0.

SUTTON PLACE. Early sixteenth century gabled manor house built by Sir Richard Weston. Motifs Italianate, but still many Gothic features in details. Often visited by Henry VIII. Queen Elizabeth slept here (1571). Seat of the Duke of Sutherland. At Guildford, Surrey, 30 miles out (train from Waterloo; Green Line, 715, from Victoria to lodge gates). Tuesday, Wednesday and Thursday (May 1-September 30), every day (July 24-September 30), 1.0-5.0.

SWAKELEY MANOR. Fair-sized mid-seventeenth century house (and therefore great rarity for London) with early wall paintings to see inside. Headquarters of the Foreign Office Sports Association. Near Uxbridge, Middlesex, 14 miles out (Piccadilly Line to Hillingdon Station). Monday to Friday, by arrangement with Secretary (RUIslip 3259).

SYON HOUSE. Some of Robert Adam's best interiors. Also pictures. Palace of Dukes of Northumberland. At Isleworth, Middlesex, 11½ miles out (train from Waterloo to Syon Lane). Wednesday to Saturday, 1.0-4.30.

WEST WYCOMBE PARK. First class mid-eighteenth century country house built about 1765 for Sir Francis Dashwood (later Baron le Despenser), founder of Medmenham Monks (with goings-on and Hell-Fire Club); also one of the founders of the Dilettanti. Lived in by Sir John Dashwood, who gave property to National Trust in 1943. Many 17th and 18th century buildings in the adjoining village, which also belongs to the National Trust. At West Wycombe, Buckinghamshire, 30 miles out (train from Marylebone and Paddington). Every day (May 12-20, July 11-August 31), except Sunday and Monday in July, 2.15-6.0.

9 am
SHOPPING

If you have resisted the lure of the *London Apprentice* or the Astors (see 8.0 a.m.) you will probably feel the first morning should be spent pottering round the shops. This can be a very pleasant experience indeed, for England is the home of quality goods, and London of the shops that display them. Neither bombs nor austerity have quite succeeded in defeating the craftsman, be he a shirt, saddle or tennis racket maker. There are more class-shops than we have any chance of mentioning: the best we can do is to make a short list. Regarding it as such, will you overlook obvious omissions? But don't get the idea that our list has been made with shut eyes and pin. The names mentioned represent quality of the highest, as understood in England; many are household names; each can be accepted as expert in his particular profession; all are of the type with whom you may safely discuss your wants without fear of the salesman trying to make a quick sale—rather your trouble will be that the salesmen tend to be delightful old gentlemen loth to part with their treasured possessions. Again, unfortunately, quality costs money to-day—more money than ever—so, if you don't expect the shops mentioned here to have cut-price standards you will sometimes have a pleasant surprise. The shops of the most " exclusive/expensive " nature (no price-tags in window), will be found in the Piccadilly-Bond Street district. Knightsbridge (Beauchamp Place) and Sloane Street have a peppering of this type; mixed with the less exclusive and chain types of shop. Oxford and Regent Streets' shop windows are, on the whole, price-tagged. A street of small shops catering for the local residents—one of every kind as in the main street of a village—is to be found in every district—even in the centre of London; further evidence that most of London is really a conglomeration of villages. Some of them still preserve strong traces of village character; Shepherd Market, just off Piccadilly (planned round a square, with pedestrian streets in the middle); Marylebone High Street; Kinnerton Street, parallel with Knightsbridge; Victoria Grove, between Kensington High Street and Gloucester Road. On the other hand, certain streets, particularly in central London, have come to specialize in one type of goods (e.g., Charing Cross Road in books—especially second-hand books). Others are given below—worth visiting to get a wide choice. Finally, of course, there are the department stores whose centre is Oxford Street. This Guide is being prepared on the principle that you know them as well as Buckingham Palace: what you want is more personal information—so not much is said about them here. Much the most interesting both as a building and for what it sells is Peter Jones of Sloane Square. Shops open about 9, close at 5.30 or 6. In main West End streets and in the City they are closed Saturday afternoons. Local shops are open on Saturdays sometimes as late as 8; close instead Wednesday or Thursday afternoons.

WHAT TO FIND WHERE

Go to St. Christopher's Place; King's Road, Chelsea; Church Street Kensington; Brompton Road and Fulham Road for second-hand furniture, antiques and old china; Lisle Street for radio spares; Kingsway for office equipment; Euston Road for engineering products; Savile Row and Hanover Square for tailoring (but for American-style ready-made men's clothes, Shaftesbury Avenue and Charing Cross Road); Kensington High Street for large drapers and household equipment; Cockspur Street (corner of Trafalgar Square), Haymarket and Lower Regent Street for shipping and travel offices; Charing Cross Road for books, music publishers, musical instruments and chemists; Tottenham Court Road for new furniture, Oxford Street, Kensington High Street and Brompton Road for department stores.

MAPS AND GUIDE-BOOKS. Find your way to Stanford's at 12-14, Long Acre, W.C.2 (turn east from Charing Cross Road at Leicester Square station; strike north-east at first crossroads). They have complete stock of maps to all scales, will spread them out on large table for you to choose the sheet you want. Alternatively, you might try Map House, 67, St. James's Street. We suggest you have a look at these: Bartholomew's *Greater London*: 21s. Excellent, very clear and detailed, but a little too heavy and clumsy to carry about, unless you have a car. Bacon's *London and Suburbs*: paper 3s. 6d., cloth 5s. Underground system and railways in separate patterns, main roads specially coloured. Stanford's *Ordnance*: London in four parts. 3s., 5s., 10s. 6d. each, according to quality. Not for detailed walking. Also available in other scales. Bacon's *The City of London*: paper 2s. 6d., cloth 4s. Cannot be bettered, but only contains the City. The following are available in handy book form with street indexes: Bartholomew's *Pocket Atlas of London*: 4s.; or Geographia's *A1 Atlas of London and Suburbs*: 2s. 6d. Coloured—6s. (paper cover), 10s. (stiff cover).

PHOTOGRAPHIC. For Leicas or other miniature cameras there is a special shop for you. The Camera Centre, 25, Burlington Arcade, the most likely people to have the very latest post-war Contax or Leica and the only ones to publish lens performances. Close behind are Lewis Newcombe Ltd. 41, Old Bond Street and R. G. Lewis, 202, High Holborn and 125, Strand. You can buy films and get them developed at most ordinary chemists. If you want them done by specialists, go to the Westminster Photographic Exchange (24, Charing Cross Road, 81, Strand, and 119, Victoria Street), quick and cheap. If you are willing to wait longer and pay more for first-class service go to Wallace Heaton, 127, New Bond Street, or Sinclair's, 3, Whitehall (Trafalgar Square end).

BOOKS, NEW AND SECOND-HAND, in Charing Cross Road and Cecil Court off it (ten bookshops); or for new books go to Bumpus (477, Oxford Street—Marble Arch end). Zwemmer's (76, Charing Cross Road, W.C.2) specialize in art books, Beaumont's (opposite them) in books about the ballet. Foyle's (119, further up, largest of all—almost too large—also has second-hand gramophone record department. In the City go to A. & F. Denny, Ltd., 33, Queen Victoria Street, E.C.4, or to Alfred Wilson, Ltd., 7, Ship Tavern Passage, E.C.3, for your reading. Hachette, the French publishers, have lately opened a French bookshop at 127, Regent Street. For French books and newspapers go also to Librairie Parisienne, 48, Old Compton Street, W.1. There are bookshops specializing in oriental literature and learning, in Great Russell Street opposite the British Museum; political bookshops are Collet's (66, Charing Cross Road, W.C.2)—red, and Fabian Society Bookshop (11, Dartmouth Street, Westminster)—pink. The bookshop at 397, Oxford Street, W.1, is open till 2 a.m. and gets French and Irish papers the same day, Italian a day late and German two days late. Famous antiquarian booksellers are Maggs Bros. (Berkeley Square, W.1)—the most exclusive of its kind in Europe: incunabula, Shakespeare folios and other collectors' items; Quaritch (Grafton Street); Francis Edwards (83, Marylebone High Street), Sotheran (Sackville Street—a few doors up from Piccadilly). David Low (not the cartoonist) in 15, Cecil Court, is very good for early engineering and scientific books. W. H. Smith & Sons' chain of shops and station bookstalls are ubiquitous—as are Wyman's.

PRINTS: TOPOGRAPHICAL AND OTHERWISE. More interesting to take home than picture post-cards, are old prints illustrating London scenes and buildings and old maps. You can get them in a good many places, but in some the prices charged are high considering that they are taken from old books, of which thousands of copies were issued, each containing dozens of prints. Best thing to do is to go to one of the print shops where they have bundles and portfolios full of them (very dusty) that you can turn over and pick what you like. Usually arranged according to cities and counties. There are shops like this at 17, Denmark Street (off Charing Cross Road), at 4, Bloomsbury Court, W.C.1 (passage leading off north side of High Holborn, just before you come to Southampton Row) and Cecil Court (off the lower part of Charing Cross Road, east side). Spencer's, 27, New Oxford Street, is rather more expensive and specializes in rarities for collectors, and so does Francis Edwards, 83, Marylebone High Street, W.1. Most of the topographical prints you buy will be engravings from books published between 1820 and 1850.

shopping arcades

London has a number of these, though not as many as the damp climate demands. Most famous is Burlington Arcade, off Piccadilly. It goes in for aristocratic haberdashery and once inside you're not allowed to run, whistle or sing, carry a large parcel, open an umbrella or wheel a pram. A beadle is always on duty to stop you if you try. Far end of the arcade was badly bombed. Most elegant example is Royal Opera Arcade (between Pall Mall East and Charles II Street): vaulted ceiling, wrought iron lamp-holders, miniature bow-fronted shops.

GENTS' TAILORING. London's reputation is founded on the work of about thirty tailors in and around Savile Row, a street, and a legend. Actually in Savile Row proper, the cloth merchants (you visit Mr. Cooper on the introduction of your tailor) have tended to push out the tailors proper, some of whom are to be found in Sackville Street or Hanover Square. Either way, it is Savile Row which stands for the great tradition of craftsmanship in clothes, built up over the centuries, and now being remorselessly broken up under the ignorant misconception that quality can't be reconciled with democracy, when the truth is democracy *must* be reconciled with quality. When you consider that the British in general and Savile Row in particular have built up a world-wide market on a reputation for high quality, it seems particularly mad that our rulers should set out to torpedo it. To counteract this, Savile Row, conservative though it is, has at last decided to act and an organization meant to catch the eye of the males in other countries has been formed under the title of The Man's Fashion Council. It consists of what are known as the Big Ten who, with one or two other famous firms, form the solid core of Savile Row tradition. Preservation of craftsmanship is one of their chief aims, for, if they lose their craftsmen, they lose their quality. That costs money. It takes seven years to train an apprentice, as machiner, cutter then designer. And when you realize that a first-class machiner may be earning £1,000 a year you will understand why it costs 50 guineas to-day to order a suit. It is usual to visit Savile Row with an introduction but this convention the tailors are not really sorry to break down. Tell the firm you select you saw their name in an American paper, that you want a tweed suit. If he turns you down it is because he is short of cloth—and that won't be an excuse. But which? Why not one of the big ten? Here they are anyway:—Benson, Perry & Whitley, Ltd., 9, Cork Street, W.1. Davies & Son, Ltd., 19, Hanover Street, W.1. Hawes & Curtis, Ltd., 43, Dover Street, W.1. James & James, 20, Sackville Street, W.1. Jones, Chalk & Dawson, 6, Sackville Street, W.1. J. B. Johnstone Ltd., 34, Sackville Street, W.1. Kilgour, French & Stanbury, Ltd., 33a, Dover Street, W.1. G. L. & C. Oaker, 31, Savile Row, W.1. Henry Poole & Co., 37, Savile Row, W.1. Sullivan, Williams & Co., Ltd., 18, Conduit Street, W.1.

For good measure we add Leslie & Roberts, 16, St. George Street, W.1. Wyser & Bryant, 11, Princes Street, Hanover Square, W.1.

LADIES' TAILORING. Also has its big ten who can be approached by the beginner in the same way as the men's. They are:—Hardy Amies, 14, Savile Row, W.1. Charles Creed, 31, Basil Street, S.W.3. Norman Hartnell, 26, Bruton Street, W.1. Lachasse 4, Farm Street, W.1. G. G. Mattli (Dress Designer), 3, Carlos Place, W.1. Digby Morton, 54, Grosvenor Hill, W.1. Peter Russell, 2, Carlos Place, W.1. Michael Sherard, 24, Connaught Street, W.2. Victor Stiebel, Jacqmar House, Grosvenor Street, W.1. Worth, 50, Grosvenor Street, W.1.

TWEED AND MATERIALS to buy in the piece for making up by your own tailor. Both men and women can go to Bill, 93, New Bond Street, W.1 (tweeds ranging from a hand-woven Harris at 21s. a yard, to a £30 a yard Vicuna); Hunt & Winterbotham, 4, Old Bond Street, W.1 (42s. Harris tweed to £5 Cheviot) and Scottish Highland Industries, 31, Beauchamp Place, S.W.3 (hand-woven tweeds and regulation clan tartans—30s. to 40s.). For women only, Jacqmar, 16, Grosvenor Street, W.1 (all materials—except for underwear—from machine-made tweeds and suitings to brocades and silks); or Harvey Nichols, Knightsbridge, S.W.1 (an even wider range of materials).

TARTAN KILTS and other Scottish specialities at Scotch House (corner of Knightsbridge and Brompton Road)—tartans of all clans; surprising how many people can lay claim to one or other of them. For our part we wish we were McLeods; would gladly contribute to laurel wreath for the unknown artist who invented those yellow symphonies.

SUITS FOR HIRE: it's quite an accepted thing to hire clothing if you go to Moss Bros., King Street, Covent Garden, whose name is a household word all over the world. They specialize in morning dress for weddings and Ascot (grey topper included), and evening dress—will fit anyone. Also hire out evening frocks to ladies and keep careful record of where their customers wear them, so they won't be embarrassed by appearing somewhere in a frock someone else was seen in the night before. Best place to buy ready-made suits and overcoats is Aquascutum, 100, Regent Street; Hawkes, 1, Savile Row, have some ready-made suits.

FOR YOUR HEAD: Go to Lock's (6, St. James's Street, S.W.1) if you want to know where bowler hats come from. The Lock bowler is celebrated for its hardness, useful if you take a toss out riding, its enceinte crown (looked at from the front), its fuzziness (brush it to make it more fuzzy) and for its feminine version with smaller brim, much affected by gentlemen who want to appear horsey. Mr. Bowler designed it, and Lock made it for Coke's gamekeepers and beaters who were in the habit of hanging their toppers on trees when the shooting started. Hence its ancient name of Coke hat. While there, notice the hat boxes. Lock's is the only shop in London that hasn't changed spiritually or architecturally since the 18th century. If, dissatisfied with these, you want your hat delivered in a brougham, you'll have to switch your allegiance to Scotts (1, Old Bond Street, W.1), whose carriages and pairs are much seen about the streets of the West End. Lock's, by the way, made the eye-shade for Nelson's blind eye.

SHIRTS, TIES, SHOES, SOCKS. Most of the shirt*makers* (who sell everything except boots) are in Jermyn Street, Piccadilly and Burlington Arcade. We support Turnbull & Asser, 71, Jermyn Street, because as well as doing good stuff they have Whistlerian peacock feather details in their shop, and several new ideas in their heads. For ready-mades the best bet is Simpson's, 202, Piccadilly, W.1, or Lillywhites, 24, Regent Street, or Fortnum & Mason's, 181, Piccadilly, W.1, but most English ready-made shirts have the wrong sort of collar—or perhaps we have the wrong sort of neck. The same three are probably the best bet for ready-made shoes (which, barring reversed hides, are in a bad spot just now) together with Randall's of 171, Regent Street, W.1, and Lotus, of 43, New Bond Street, W.1 (ask for 1084, 1050, and particularly 1110). Shoe*makers* are: Lobb, 26, St. James's Street; Maxwell, 9, Dover Street; McAfee, 38, Dover Street; Bartley, 493, Oxford Street, and Peal, 487, Oxford Street (originators of patent leather and makers of the jack boots worn by the Life Guards), who have a particularly good *polishable* waterproof dressing (Peal's W.P. Dressing).

SPORTS EQUIPMENT. Most big stores have a sports department. The real specialists are Lillywhites (24, Lower Regent Street). Pro in attendance for tennis rackets. Famous also for sports clothes (don't miss their Windcheaters). Sports-gear shops: Wisden's, 15, Gt. Newport Street; Holden, 232, Baker Street; Jack Hobbs, 59, Fleet Street (kept by second most famous English cricketer). For sport as opposed to sports go for fishing tackle to Ogden Smith, 62, St. James's Street, or Hardy's, 15, Pall Mall; for guns, James Purdey, 57, S. Audley Street, and Vaughan's (33, Bedford Street, Strand); for saddles to Champion & Wilton (457/9, Oxford Street, W.1); for bridles and rugs to George Parker (12, Upper St. Martin's Lane); for hunting crops and other leather goods to Swaine, Adeney, Brigg & Sons (185, Piccadilly, W.1); for riding boots and spurs to Maxwell (8 and 9, Dover Street, W.1), Bartley (493, Oxford Street, W.1); for breeches to Tautz (9, Stratton Street, W.1); for jodhpurs to Huntsman, 11, Savile Row.

PERFUMES. J. Floris have been at 89, Jermyn Street, S.W.1, since 1730 (Nelson once had rooms above). Perfumed George IV, 1820 onwards. Mr. Michael will tell you about their special No. 127 for men—first made in 1930's for a Russian aristocrat living in Paris. There is the rose geranium shaving soap, too, in those nice round wooden bowls with lids. For ladies, English scents, not a bit expensive. In case you're interested, we prefer Honeysuckle. The attendants at Floris will present your change on a cushion as if they were Archbishop of Canterbury, you King of England. If Floris haven't got quite what you want, try Mr. Thomas, of Eton fame, at 11, Duke Street, St. James's, S.W.1, or Truefitt & Hill, 23, Old Bond Street, where you can get a particularly telling hair grease *crème cosmétique* (known to initiates as shrimp paste). Hair cuts as well at either of the last two places. Also for gents' hairdressing, Trumper, 9, Curzon Street, and Topper, 17-18, Old Bond Street.

new

Modern shops can be interesting architecturally too, though most of them are not. Two large stores of exciting modern design are Simpson's (Piccadilly) and Peter Jones (Sloane Square). Among small shops the best designed are some of the recent travel offices: South Africa, 70, Piccadilly, W.1; Swiss, 458/9, Strand, W.C.2 (Trafalgar Square); Swedish, 21/2, Coventry Street, W.1, though the last two are somewhat spoilt externally by a poor standard of window display; Others worth looking for are the newly-decorated Dolcis shoe shops. Other chain stores that go in for a high standard of designs are Jaeger's, Cresta and Richard shops (all for women's wear).

MODERN FURNITURE. Try Dunn's of Bromley, twenty-five minutes from Charing Cross but well worth the time and effort. Geoffrey Dunn, himself a designer, is almost alone among manufacturers in actively encouraging young designers of modern furniture, fabrics, pottery. Also at Story's, 49, Kensington High Street, W.8. Amidst a welter of expensive mediocrity there is one refreshing oasis: the work of the new Story Design Group. Heal's, pioneers of the arts and crafts movement, still continue this tradition in Tottenham Court Road, while if you brave the pompous façade of Liberty's in Regent Street you will be rewarded by a good selection of modern fabrics. For a cross-section of what's new in wallpapers go north of Oxford Street to Cole's, 18, Mortimer Street, W.1, who have a magnificent collection of old papers as well; Sanderson's, 52, Berners Street, W.1, and Line's, 214, Tottenham Court Road. Lamps and lampshades? Try Primavera in Sloane Street for the Scandinavian (Le Klint) angle, the Lighting Centre in Knightsbridge and the Merchant Adventurers, Portland Road, W.11.

CHINA AND GLASS. For the china, Wedgwood (historic name) at 34, Wigmore Street, W.1; for both, Goode's, 19, South Audley Street, W.1, and Lawley's, 150, Regent Street, W.1. For the best *modern* china and glass, Peter Jones, Sloane Square, and John Lewis, Oxford Street; Heal's, Tottenham Court Road.

GLASSES, meaning spectacles—George Odell, 30, King Street, S.W.1; Hamblin, 15, Wigmore Street; Negretti & Zambra, 122,

Regent Street, famous meteorological instrument makers.

GLASSES, meaning field glasses—Wallace Heaton, 127, New Bond Street, W.1.

KITCHEN EQUIPMENT. There's a famous shop in Victoria Street (Staines, 94, near Victoria station), full of pots and pans and gadgets of all kinds, but you may find it more amusing to go to one of the little shops in Soho (Old Compton Street, Greek Street, etc.) that supply restaurateurs. Specially good for chef's knives, pepper-mills, copper coffee-pots.

CURIOS AND JEWELLERY. A very difficult subject since either the goods are cheap and phoney, or genuine and worth a ransom. Cameo Corner (26, Museum Street, W.C.1, on the right after leaving Great Russell Street) is worth visiting for souvenirs not stamped " Festival of Britain," but they are not exactly cheap. You'll probably be served by the proprietor, cloaked in purple velvet. For things like heraldic emblems, try Strongi'th'arm's, 13, Dover Street (Mr. Hutchins and Mr. Groves), an ancient institution pleasant to know not only for its quality (which is high) but for its name. Another name not unknown to you for jewellery will be Cartier (get your engagement ring here). For bric-à-brac the best bet is the antique shops.

AUCTION ROOMS. London has two world-famous auctioneers: Sotheby's (34, New Bond Street) and Christie's (Spencer House, 27, St. James's Place, ancestral home of Earls Spencer, fine eighteenth century mansion by Vardy, overlooking Green Park). Both sell antique furniture, pictures, carpets, silver, china, jewellery, books, etc.—larger collectors' pieces and the sales are mostly attended by dealers. But anyone can go—it's an interesting spectacle—though take care not to put in a bid by mistake. Dealers bid by signs almost imperceptible to anyone but the auctioneer, and an unintended blink of the eyelid may land you with a huge Victorian oil-painting and a case of fish-knives at some hundreds of guineas. Sales are announced in the *Telegraph* (Mondays) and *Times* (Tuesdays). Printed catalogues can be obtained and the items to be sold can usually be inspected for three days beforehand.

LEATHER. Tattersall's (world-famous horse mart, Knightsbridge end of Brompton Road) no longer exists—it has been turned into a furniture warehouse and the charming architecture ruined—but Tom Hill's shop (26, just opposite) still sells all kinds of horsey leather goods—riding boots, gaiters, gloves; also dog-collars and leashes. West End opposite number is Swaine, Adeney, Brigg & Sons for all the horsey leather goods (see above) or, for bags and cases, Drew's of 33, Regent Street.

TRUNKS, BAGS AND UMBRELLAS. Don't tell Jermyn Street, but you can buy these second-hand at any shops that dispose of un-claimed lost property—mostly from the railways. (103, New Oxford Street, W.C.1; 359, Oxford Street, W.1; 87, Regent Street, W.1; 150, Strand, W.C.2; 3, Hudson Place, adjoining Victoria Station, S.W.1; and 96A, Victoria Street, S.W.1).

PIPES. The things you smoke, Inderwick, 45, Carnaby Street, W.1, the King's pipe shop, and of course there is Dunhill's of white spot fame, 30, Duke Street, St. James's.

old

If you're interested in shops, not only to buy at, but to look at, visit some of the little old shops left over from the eighteenth century: Lock's, St. James's Street (see under HATS) with its window exhibit of antique models, including a red trilby ordered by an Indian prince for his bearers; Fribourg and Treyer, Haymarket (tobacco and snuff—founded 1720); a charming row of bay-windowed shops (actually early nineteenth century) in Woburn Walk. Less like museum specimens, but charming of their kind, are Savory & Moore's chemist's shop, 143, New Bond Street, and the Three Sugar Loaves and Crown, 14, Creechurch Lane, E.C.3, one of the first firms to import tea into England (1650; cost £6-£10 a pound) and also sold some of the tea later thrown into Boston harbour which began the war of American independence.

PROVISIONS AND GROCERIES can be got round the corner from your neighbour, from Soho, Marylebone High Street, and the department stores. For the mouth-watering variety like smoked salmon, potted shrimps, foie gras, brandied nectarines, strawberries preserved in wine, there are two great centres, Fortnum & Mason, Piccadilly (for cheque book shoppers), and Selfridge's Food Store (in Orchard Street, behind main Oxford Street building) for those who want unheard of herbs or rare peppers. And for ready-to-eat extravagances, cold birds or variegated salads, don't overlook the counters of Lyons' Corner Houses at Coventry Street and Strand. For those who are staying in furnished rooms and want to feed themselves exotically or cheaply, Soho (London's Latin quarter) is a happy hunting ground. You'll find dozens of small shops selling food of all nations, cheeses, breads, wines, macaroni, dried fish, herbs, spices. Explore Old Compton, Brewer, Greek, Rupert Streets for exotic things. Noodles, for instance, sweet-sour, bean sprouts, bamboo shoots, from Shanghai Emporium, 118, Greek Street; cods-roe-butter, Littaur cheese with paprika, chive and garlic and kippers smoked in oak smoke, from Hamburger's, 1, Brewer Street, W.1, everything Italian from A. & J. Del Monico, 64, Old Compton Street, W.1, and G. Parmigiani, 36A, Old Compton Street, W.1, and continental varieties of bread from Mr. Rosin, 27, Peter Street, and Floris Bakeries, 24, Brewer Street. Some very good coffee can be had in tins from Lyons—Lyons *French* coffee with the chicory unremoved—and the yoghourt addict will find the Express Dairies (branches everywhere) very handy. The amateur cook for whom this sort of thing is a new experience may want to try his hand at some special sauces—if so, get *Cooking with Wine* by Nell Heaton (Faber & Faber, 8s. 6d.). If you are northwards of Oxford Street, Marylebone High Street will be found a rewarding alternative to Soho. If south of Piccadilly, the great cheese shop is Paxton & Whitfield, at 93, Jermyn Street, S.W.1.

RUSSIAN CAVIAR merchant is the title of a little shop in Orange Street (turning east off Haymarket): W. G. White, No. 17. Also imports bêche-de-mer, sun-dried turtle and Chinese bird-nests for making soup.

CHOCOLATES. De Bry, 191, Brompton Road, 1910 French teashop atmosphere (whiff of Promenade des Anglais) or Bendick's, 151, New Bond Street, W.1 (and many other branches).

WINE MERCHANTS. Berry Bros. & Rudd, 3, St. James's Street. Shop built 1731. First shop styled itself as Italian warehousemen (grocers dealing mainly in spice, tea, coffee, and wine) from which era survives the sign which hangs outside, " the Sign of the Sugar Loaf ". The smaller scales that hang in the shop (17th century craftsmanship, and so perfectly balanced that they will swing for 12 minutes) were used to weigh merchandise. The other pair have always been used to weigh customers, a unique and not abating feature which they are perfectly willing to oblige with today. But more interesting are the books recording the weights of famous and infamous since 1765. Notice the change to " Sign of the Coffee Mill." This side of the business moved and is now Fry's in Duke Street, St. James's. Look out for the slope of the floor, due to foundations being built direct on the clay soil. Old wine bottles, biggest collection in the country and if you want to know more about the subject get the book by Sheila Ruggles-Brise. An almost complete duplicate wine cellar of the Queen's Dolls House; labelled bottles (containing wine) twelfth full size.

FLOWERS in the West End may be got off barrow boys and old ladies at corners if you have time; or have them sent by Moyses Stevens, 146, Victoria Street, S.W.1 (also night service), and Lansdowne House, Berkeley Square, W.1.

highly specialized

Shops worth a visit for their uniqueness and often richly decorative appearance (though you're not likely to want to buy anything) are: Gerrard's, 61, College Place, Camden Town, N.W.1 (for stuffed bears, tigers, foxes' masks, fish, birds, dogs, and etc.—showroom and workshops surrounding courtyard); Clement Clarke, Wigmore Street (trays of glass eye-balls in the window, all colours, some, with alarming verisimilitude, made a little bloodshot); Hooper & Co., Ltd. at the top of St. James' Street (for coach work—some of the splendid private carriages they built can be seen behind the upper windows of the impressive plate-glass façade, but now they concentrate on the body-work of luxury motorcars); Morley's, 56, Old Brompton Road, S.W.7 (for harps); Henry Starck, 12, Kentish Town Road (bagpipes—family firm, Victorian atmosphere, first-floor workshop 100 years old, originally made police truncheons); Adam Rouilly, 18, Fitzroy Street (for skeletons: they're imported from abroad for use of medical students and others—price 10 to 15 guineas—female skeletons the more difficult to get).

NATURALIST. Watkins & Doncaster, of 36, Strand, have everything for the bug hunter: setting boards, killing-bottles, and butterfly nets. Books on natural history will be found at Rowland Ward, 167, Piccadilly.

STAMP AND OTHER COLLECTORS will find the shops they want in William IV Street (near Trafalgar Square), Strand (Stanley Gibbons is at No. 391), Broadway (Westminster) and—most remarkable of all, Victoria Street, where the Collector's Shop at No. 75a stocks anything people are peculiar enough to collect in numbers above a hundred: not only foreign stamps but bus and tram tickets (proprietor John A. Rayner will only buy these if they're of 8d. value or over), match-box and hotel labels, processed cheese labels (one of the newest crazes), milk bottle tops, razor blade and cigarette packets, orange and apple wrappers (over a thousand, all different), theatre programmes since 1880. Mr. Rayner has compiled a collectors' and dealers' directory.

YACHTING EQUIPMENT. Get all you want, if you're going sailing (except the boat to sail in) at Beale's, 194, Shaftesbury Avenue (High Holborn end). "Yacht stores and ships chandler" it's called: everything from books on navigation to binnacle lamps.

PAINTS AND BRUSHES for artists: several shops in King's Road, Chelsea; Reeves (lower end of Charing Cross Road); Winsor & Newton (51, Rathbone Place, off Oxford Street); Lechertier Barbe (Jermyn Street); Geo. Rowney & Co., 10 and 11, Percy Street.

MODEL THEATRES. Benjamin Pollock (16, Little Russell Street, near British Museum, W.C.1) successors to the original Hoxton shop, immortalized by Robert Louis Stevenson in "Penny Plain and Twopence Coloured", still sell the penny sheets; also the theatres they go with.

MODEL RAILWAYS, and ships and aeroplanes. Too beautifully made (and too expensive) to be regarded as toys, are the models to be seen at Bassett-Lowke's in Holborn (112, High Holborn, W.C.1, almost opposite top of Kingsway)—world-famous model-railway specialists. Absolutely true to scale and complete in every detail, you can get every item of railway equipment from track, locomotives, rolling stock and signals to station-advertisements, auto-slot machines, milk-churns, luggage to lie around on the platforms and even the passengers.

CHESSMEN. For chess players there's Emil's in Burlington Arcade with a window that's full of chessmen, a wonderfully various collection of sets is on view: old and modern; Chinese, Persian, Indian, European; ivory, bone and wood. The proprietor is very learned on the subject.

SUNDIALS AND MANTELPIECES. If you collect antiques of the larger kind, visit Crowther's (282, North End Road—near Olympia) and come away with a real Adam mantelpiece, a garden fountain and a set of oak balusters from an Elizabethan staircase. They buy the bits and pieces from old houses when they are demolished or modernized; the collection in stock—surrealistically juxtaposed in their warehouse—has to be seen to be believed.

PAWNBROKERS. All the best people pawn their watches at T. M. Sutton, 156, Victoria Street, or Vaughan's, 39, Strand.

FOR CHILDREN. Best known children's outfitters are Daniel Neal's, who have a shop in Portman Square, and Fortnum and Mason. Most Oxford and Regent Street drapery stores have a children's department. For unusually well designed TOYS (especially the educational kind), go to Paul & Marjorie Abbatt, 94, Wimpole Street, W.1 (just north of Oxford Street), spacious modern shop—also toy department at Heal's, Tottenham Court Road. Biggest toy-shop—almost a children's department store—is Hamley's, 200, Regent Street, W.1, good for games and mechanical toys.

miscellany

Miscellaneous shops of architectural interest for one reason or another: Chappell's (50, New Bond Street)—the neo-Gothic façade was designed by Owen Jones, also one of the architects to the Great Exhibition, 1851, responsible for the colour inside the Crystal Palace; Twining's (216, Strand, opposite Law Courts) tea merchants—miniature shop entrance with heraldic decoration of great charm; Asprey's, the Bond Street jewellers, is a very refined specimen of the Victorian glass shop-front and Ellisdon's (246, High Holborn)—a good specimen of the Victorian all-glass façade; the charmingest bay window in London is on the first floor of No. 32, Old Bond Street.

10 am
LONDON AT WORK

You're in London on holiday, but it's not a holiday for Londoners, so why not see them at work? Here we list a few places where people will be delighted to show you around. Take this opportunity to see how Parliament works, the law courts function, your motor car is made, your milk bottled, your money coined, your mail sorted. Trades and professions inevitably congregate in certain districts—and a discreet tour will be rewarding. Here are just a few of the trade localities:— cars, Warren Street, Great Portland Street, W.1; consulting engineers, Victoria Street, S.W.1; film companies, Wardour Street, W.1; furniture, East End, E.1; furs, Garlick Hill, Upper Thames Street, E.C.4; hairdressers' requirements, Soho, W.1; hop exchange, Southwark, S.E.1; leather, Bermondsey, S.E.1; linen, Russia Row, E.C.2; printing, Fleet Street, E.C.4; produce (butter, cheese, eggs), Tooley Street, S.E.1; produce (tea, coffee, spices), Mincing Lane, E.C.3; shipping and insurance, Leadenhall Street, Fenchurch Street, E.C.3; textiles, St. Paul's, E.C.4; wool merchants, Golden Square, W.1.

THE LAW

Old Bailey (Central Criminal Court), E.C.1. See the law at work. You are allowed into the public galleries of the two courts at 10.0 and 2.0. Accommodation limited to about 60. Length of queue (outside a little door in Newgate Street) depends on importance of case, but if it's nothing special allow half an hour before the session. If you're one of the first you will get a grandstand view from near the ceiling of No. 1 Court. Less lucky to be in No. 2 Court, where spectators are on the same level as the rest. You don't need a ticket to get in, and for that reason if the case is important you will not get in twice on the same day. If you want to see just the building, then go along to the entrance in Old Bailey (also name of a street) just before 11.0 on a Saturday morning. You will be shown round in a party.

Magistrates' Courts. Provide much material for the evening

papers, in fact a regular column (*Evening News*). Go and see for yourself. Bow Street, W.C.2, and Marlborough Street, W.1, are the most accessible and interesting. Open 10.0 to 5.0 with time off for lunch. You can get in quite easily if you get there at opening time, unless the case is a popular one. There are fifteen courts altogether in the London area (listed in the telephone directory).

Parliament

To get a close-up view of Attlee and Churchill in battle or one of the Ministers answering questions on yet another cut, go to the House of Commons. Admission to the Strangers' Gallery, while the House of Commons is sitting in the Chamber (bombed, rebuilt and opened last year), if English, by writing to your M.P. (about three weeks in advance); if from abroad, from your Embassy or Dominion House. Or you can go on spec. Queue outside St. Stephen's door at 2.0 (for 3.30), on Fridays at 11.0, and you may be one of the lucky 156. You can stay as long as you like and if in need will get a re-admission pass valid for half an hour. You may see over Houses of Parliament without any awkward preliminaries on Saturdays, 10.0-3.0. Go to the Norman Porch (ask a policeman where that is) and you will be routed through and allowed out at St. Stephen's. It will take you an hour.

local government

Attend a Council meeting at County Hall. The 150 members will, in the manner of a miniature Parliament, be discussing the more intimate subjects, housing, schools, health, catering, the affairs of a city. There will be an agenda for you. You will probably get in if you go on spec., the public gallery holds 60. To see over the County Hall get in touch with the Clerk of the Council. Main entrance in Belvedere Road, S.E.1. Council meetings, alternate Tuesdays, 2.30.

stock exchange

Just a very few people will be permitted to see the Stock Exchange in action. The best time to see the house is about 11.0 (although it opens at 9.30) Mondays to Fridays. Apply when you get there to the Financial Secretary and you will be directed to the first floor of 23, Throgmorton Street, E.C.2.

think of a letter

The most interesting Post Office is Mount Pleasant sorting office for all letters to the country. Vast, and impersonal as the outside of an envelope. You will be shown around by sorters, who will answer all your questions. No tips allowed.

Points of interest, the Blind Letter Corner (that letter—the address that you didn't quite catch). In the parcels section Heartbreak Corner (that package—if only I had a bit more string, but never mind !). You will be shown the post office railway, little automatic monsters rushing from one station to another all by themselves, to be seen well below ground under the bright fluorescent lighting of the station. Rosebery Avenue, E.C.1. The best time, between 5.30 and 7.30 at night. Write to the Divisional Controller's office, Mount Pleasant.

motor-car production

Visit Ford's at Dagenham, and save yourself five other visits, because while you are there you can visit the power station, coke oven, jetty, blast furnace, foundry and three assembly lines, all little industries in themselves. You will also get a good look at the Zephyr and Consul and their brand new production line. On two other lines, tractors, cars, vans and lorries. Don't be shy. There are 17 guides and they handle up to 350 visitors a day (of course if you've been to Detroit, you're not interested). Two tours per day, at 9.30 and 2.0. The afternoon visit is the more leisurely and you get a cup of tea into the bargain. Ring up Visits Dept. (Rainham 3000) to fix the details. If you make the date a few days ahead, you may get a guide more or less to yourself. No visits Saturdays or Sundays. No tips necessary, no cameras allowed, nor junior if he is under ten. You will probably be asked to go to the Ford's Sports Pavilion in Kent Avenue. (District Line, or Central Line, changing to District at Mile End, to Dagenham Heathway and 175 bus from there to Prince's Cinema, and then 3 minutes walk; allow a good hour.)

music

Radios, gramophones, records and irons are all made by His Master's Voice. Here's your chance to see the inside of a wireless set, and a record when it's just a ball of shellac. Write to Mr. Bowen, E.M.I. Factories, Ltd., Blyth Road, Hayes, Middlesex, stating alternative dates and you will be shown around. Tours take two hours. Tea at the end.

milk-o

Visit a bottling plant. A world of clattering milk bottles and significant colour. Perhaps the United Dairies one in South Lambeth Road, S.W.8. All colours on your milk bottle caps indicate a grade. Ask them. Inside the plant, the stainless steel tanks (the only practicable metal in which to keep milk), the red and blue, steam and water pipes, the boiler room, the smell of warm milk, the enormous bottle washer, the surgeon-like men who stand over the filling machines, 4,000,000 bottles a week. Public Relations Dept. (BAY: 2400).

bell casting

Mears and Stainbank. In business since 1570. Bells cast include Great Tom of St. Paul's (the original agreement for casting still exists), and Big Ben. Visitors shown over between hours of 10.0 and 4.0 Mondays to Fridays. Write or telephone to arrange time of visit. If you don't know how to get there, firm will send you a small printed map with nearest stations marked. 34, Whitechapel Road, E.1. (BIS: 2599).

pottery

The Fulham Pottery. Granted a charter in 1671 by Charles

II, still going strong. Started by John Dwight (you may have heard of Dwight ware), produced first " utility " pottery, then called Cologne Ware. In production such diverse items as vases, filters and general stone ware. They provide modelling clay and also have facilities for firing other people's work. 210, New King's Road, S.W.6. Contact Mr. Cheavin or Mr. West. (Previous notice required.)

glass works

Whitefriars Glass Works, founded in 1680, on the site of the White Friars monastery (Fleet Street), where it remained until 1923, when it moved to Wealdstone. Your tour, lasting about 1½ hours, starts at the melting furnaces, where you will see raw materials (mainly sand, red lead, potash and saltpetre) melting in enormous beehive-like pots. After seeing the raw materials being mixed, you will be taken to the Glass House (not the Army variety) where you will see all the shaping and blowing processes being carried out by the " gaffer," " footmaker," " servitor " and " taker-in." Get the gaffer to explain the meaning of " tease-hole," " cavillator," " moyls " and the many other strange words he uses. Watch the skill with which these craftsmen shape the glass into tubing and chemical glassware (a major part of their output) and vases, table and other domestic glassware—mostly export. Tour finishes in stained glass department (which in its time has executed designs by Rossetti, Burne-Jones, William Morris), where you may get a preview of the Temple Church window on which they will be starting work this summer. Write to Messrs. James Powell & Sons (Whitefriars) Limited, Whitefriars Glass Works, Tudor Road, Wealdstone, Middlesex.

11 am
THEY BUILD

There will be amongst you visitors concerned with the building industry, especially architects, who might like to see what London has to offer in the way of building and its component industries. All the people listed below have agreed to show you round their works and showrooms if you have a bona-fide interest in the building game. There are many others who will welcome you at their showrooms or works but space only permits us to print a very limited list. (Pay a visit to the Building Centre, described by us under 2 p.m., it is in fact a museum, where amazingly obliging people will give you all the additional information you may want.)

THE LMBA IS IN TOUCH, through the National Federation, with members of all building associations in the Dominions, offering to assist them in every way possible to see British building methods on the sites. Visits are to be arranged to building sites in London, building contractors' works, joinery shops, etc., and similar arrangements will be available through the various Regional Federations of the National Federation throughout England, Wales and Scotland. So if you are an architect or in the building trade and want to see what London is doing, get in touch with G. H. A. Hughes, Director of the London Master Builders Association at 47, Bedford Square, W.C.1 (MUS. 3891).

To recognize PRACTICALLY ANY WOOD on earth, go to the timber library (4,000 items) of the Timber Development Association Ltd., also to observe new timbers being tested for their properties and research into the further uses of timber. Ring first; head office and research and information Bureau: 21, College Hill, E.C.4. Telephone: City 4771.

CHEAPSIDE WAS FIRST PAVED in 1871, the popular surface now is "Rock-non-skid." Then and now carried out by Val de Travers Asphalte Paving Company Ltd. Also manufacture natural rock asphalt for roofs and coloured asphalt for floors. Works at Sun Wharf, Creekside, Deptford. London office: 21, Old Bailey, E.C.4. Telephone: City 7001.

DEMONSTRATIONS GIVEN of the new "Ductube" process of providing continuous ducts in concrete structures and pre-cast concrete products by Wiggins-Sankey Ltd., builders' merchants and roofing contractors. London office and show-

rooms: Rosebank Wharf, Lysia Street, Fulham, S.W.6. Telephone: Fulham 1250.

TO SEE HOW SOME FLOORS ARE MADE, visit the Armstrong Cork Co., makers of Accotile Flooring, who will not only show you round their factory, but will also take you to any building being installed with their flooring. London offices and showroom: Bush House, Aldwych, W.C.2 (Chancery 6281).

GAS WATER HEATERS are made by Ascot Gas Water Heaters, Ltd. London office: 43, Park Street, W.1. Telephone: Grosvenor 4491, with whom you will be able to fix a visit to the London factory.

MANUFACTURERS OF ASBESTOS CEMENT and pre-stressed concrete products are the Atlas Stone Company, Ltd. Their London office: Artillery House, Artillery Row, Westminster, S.W.1. Telephone: Abbey 3081.

MANUFACTURERS OF 'BAKELITE' PLASTICS. Bakelite Ltd., London office and showrooms: 18, Grosvenor Gardens, S.W.1. Telephone: Sloane 9911.

TO SEE GLASS in all its shapes and forms, as steps (which just go to show how elastic glass can be) or as electric insulators or walls to fish tanks, visit the showrooms of Pilkington Bros. Ltd. at Selwyn House, Cleveland Row, S.W.1. The opening of these showrooms was one of the architectural events of 1950, well worth seeing as a very good piece of interior decoration. Telephone: Whitehall 5672.

HAND-PRINTED and machined wallpaper, contemporary wallpapers, all kinds of them, from the cheapest machine-printed to imported hand-painted Chinese, with ones from Sweden and France, silk flocks, woodgrain, and special export patterns for the American market. All this at the showrooms of Arthur Sanderson & Sons, Berners Street, W.1. Telephone: Museum 7800.

GONE ARE THE DAYS when the only way of getting at a building was by boards supported on a crazy framework of poles tied with rope. Scaffolding (Gt. Britain) Ltd. are past masters at the art of encasing a building in shining metal tubes (Victoria Tower, Houses of Parliament, a fine example). Head office and factory: Willow Lane, Mitcham, Surrey. Telephone:

Mitcham 3400. In the same line of business, Mills Scaffold Company Ltd., London works: Trussley Works, Hammersmith Grove, W.6. Telephone: Riverside 5026.

ELECTRIC CLOCKS and industrial instruments, Smiths English Clocks Ltd. Head office and works: Cricklewood Works, N.W.2. Telephone: Gladstone 6464 (R. B. MacMorran, Public Relations Officer).

CONSTRUCTIONAL ENGINEERS are Structural & Mechanical Development Engineers Ltd., Head office: Buckingham Avenue, Slough, Bucks. Telephone: Slough 23212.

CELLULOSE LACQUER and synthetic finishes. Manufacturers are Cellon Ltd. Factory and Research Laboratories: Richmond Road, Kingston-on-Thames. Telephone: Kingston 1234.

That DECEPTIVELY SOLID WALL may in fact consist of insulating board or wallboard, made in fact of bagasse (sugar cane fibre) and wood fibre. You can see how these boards are made at:— Celotex Ltd., works and offices: North Circular Road, Stonebridge Park, N.W.10. Telephone: Elgar 5717, to see round.

Manufacture EVERYTHING FROM WINDOW PANES to the lighthouse on top of the shot tower, Chance Brothers Ltd., London office and showrooms: 28, St. James's Square, S.W.1. Telephone: Whitehall 1603.

THE RESEARCH COUNCIL for the design and production of solid fuel appliances is the Coal Utilisation Joint Council. London office: 13, Grosvenor Gardens, S.W.1. Telephone: Victoria 1534. Visits to the Council's Training Centre, Vauxhall Walk, S.E.11, arranged on Thursdays and Fridays of each week. Contact should be made with Mr. F. W. Brick, Publicity Officer of the Council.

Visit the SHOWROOMS OF CRITTALL and see everything in steel windows and doors, in size from a sliding folding door 12 ft. long to a larder window. First visit their showroom, and then if still interested you may visit the factory in Essex by arrangement, any Wednesday. Crittall Manufacturing Company, Ltd., 210, High Holborn, W.C.1. Telephone: Holborn 6612.

BRIDGES ARE MADE by Dawnays Ltd. They are also structural engineers. Visits to their Welwyn Garden City works and fabrication depot arranged through their London office: 54, Victoria Street, S.W.1. Telephone: Victoria 1541.

DO YOU REMEMBER that last seat that was so comfortable? It may have been of " Dunlopillo " (latex foam rubber), a great contribution to the comfort of M.P.'s at long debates. Visit the showrooms of the Dunlop Rubber Co., at 19/20, New Bond Street, W.1, for a moving exhibition showing the manufacture of foam rubber, several examples of mattresses and various seats. Telephone: Mayfair 9040.

VISIT THE SHOWROOMS of an interior decorator and furnisher (Gill & Reigate Ltd.) at Arlington House, Arlington Street, S.W.1. Telephone: Mayfair 6257.

LIFTS are made by Hammond & Champness Ltd. London factory: Gnome House, Blackhorse Lane, Walthamstow, E.17. Telephone: Larkswood 1071.

Makers of METAL WINDOWS, doors and pressed steel products are Henry Hope & Sons Ltd. London showrooms: 17, Berners Street, W.1. Telephone: Museum 8412.

THE TECHNICAL SERVICE and Development Laboratories of the I.C.I. Plastics Division may be visited at Tewin Road, Welwyn Garden City. Telephone: Welwyn Garden 3344.

GAS LIGHTING AND HEATING equipment and gas incinerators are made by William Sugg & Company Ltd. London office, showrooms and works: Ranelagh Works, Chapter Street, Victoria, S.W.1. Telephone: Victoria 3211.

To see ARCHITECTURAL METAL WORKERS, telephone the Morris Singer Company (Reliance 4129) at their London bronze foundry, Dorset Road, Clapham, S.W.8.

WILLIAM MORRIS & COMPANY recently completed a window for Mbarara, first stained glass window in Uganda. They are now working on the west window of St. Matthew's Church, Auckland, New Zealand. Six artists at work painting, firing, designing; if you are particularly interested you will be taken to Stoke Newington, 5 miles away, to see the assembly shop. Wm. Morris & Co., Designers and Manufacturers of Ecclesiastical Stained Glass Windows, London studio: Hope House, Great Peter Street, Westminster, S.W.1. Telephone: Abbey 2393.

London DEMONSTRATION SHOWROOMS of the North Thames Gas Board, 30, Kensington Church Street, Kensington, W.8. Telephone: Western 8141.

12 noon
WEST ENDSCAPE

Much later on, when you salute tomorrow (at midnight to be precise), we try to say something about the Festival which others will not say. Right now we take it you are fed up with the whole thing, tired of modern architecture,* sick of abstracts, and significant form, though not,

---

* If not, read Ian McCallum's POCKET GUIDE TO MODERN BUILDINGS IN LONDON. (Architectural Press, 3s. 6d.)

we hope, of townscape. If so, retrace your steps to lunch and the West End by a route that will give you a good cross-section through 18th-century London.

AWAY FROM IT ALL

Leave the Festival by Chicheley Street Gate and instead of crossing Westminster Bridge walk along the riverside foot-path under St. Thomas's Hospital (opposite the Houses of Parliament) to Lambeth Palace (stunning Tudor set-up) whence you get the best-ever view of the H. of P. Before crossing, turn left, then first right into an alley which takes you through the practice yard of the London Fire Brigade. If you're in luck they'll be climbing the fire tower and squirting hoses all over the place, but to the student of London, as we know you are by now, the real point of your exercise is to read the name of the fire brigade's back alley which you will find is called Lambeth High Street. Why? Because, believe it or not, it *is* Lambeth High Street—that's why you can get into the L.F.B.'s back yard. Nothing gives a clearer picture of the staggering changes in London's silhouette than this street name-plate with all it tells of change and decay. Lambeth Walk by the way is parallel with you now, a hundred yards or so inland from the river.

over the river

Now go back to Lambeth Bridge (only a few yards away), cross, go down Horseferry Road, turn first right down Dean Bradley Street into blitzed Smith Square, which contains (in centre) burnt-out shell of St. John's Church, Thomas Archer architect, completed 1728. (Queen Anne did not like his first design, kicked over her stool in anger and said " Make it look like that.") Nearest English architecture ever got to full-blooded Baroque, and impressive, in its present state. Thence through Lord North Street, across Great Peter Street into Cowley Street, Barton Street and Great College Street, centre of charming Georgian residential quarter of quiet streets and small houses, many occupied by M.P.s, through archway to Dean's Yard (note trees).

Westminster Abbey

Don't go straight through Dean's Yard, nice though it is, but at next archway on right, turn into Westminster School Yard and then left at bottom under another archway which will take you right into Dark Cloister of Westminster Abbey (if, before leaving the school yard, you can find a friendly looking native, try and get him to show you Inigo Jones' staircase in Ashburnham House—part of Westminster School—and store up for your townscape notebook the terrific scene of the Victoria Tower of the Houses of Parliament rising over the gardens, remembering if you can at same time that this is the centre of the metropolis.) Little Cloister (right) is little known, approached by a magnificent tunnel. Return, via tunnel, and so to main cloister, whence by a side door you enter Abbey which, by a strange paradox, is Gothic museum of one of Europe's great collections of Baroque sculpture in the shape of the monuments to the famous dead. You *must* see the Nightingale Monument and don't miss Wade, Newton and Hargrave.

Queen Anne's Gate

Leave by the North door and cross Parliament Square, use-lessly remodelled this year, left into Great George Street (notice specially No. 12, one of the best 18th-century small buildings in London), straight on through Storey's Gate (Joe Thorn, who has been in the parks for 40 years, looks after this gate and Queen Anne's Gate), into Park, up Birdcage Walk, look out for the passage on the left, Cockpit Steps site of the old Cockpit, demolished 1812—see diary of Boswell, who, incidentally, lived in Downing Street (home of Prime Ministers) in 1763; mount steps and turn right into Queen Anne's Gate (Park Street this end, Queen's Square beyond on old maps), finest existing example of Queen Anne street-architecture; passing No. 12 (National Club) the only other known job of Elmes, architect of St. George's-Hall-Liverpool fame; passing also statue of Queen Anne herself, London's leading mystery sculpture since nothing whatever is known about it or its sculptor, though it is one of London's best and none the worse for the stones small boys were encouraged to throw at it for a hundred years, in the belief that it was Bloody Mary. Past the offices of the National Trust, then out by Queen Anne's Gate into St. James's Park. As you go look back at Queen Anne's Mansions, London's first skyscraper, built to annoy Queen Victoria, whose minions had previously forbidden the syndicate in-volved to build on Crown Lands within the sight of Bucking-ham Palace (the thirteen floors are entirely brick-on-brick construction. Indirectly brought about the law limiting the height of buildings).

into the park

Before crossing Birdcage Walk read the rules and regula-tions. If you can't be bothered, at least be warned by us of one of the rules, which is that you may not wash clothes, or dip your head in the canal. The park was enclosed by Henry VIII and allegedly laid out by Le Notre (Greenwich Park and Versailles) for Charles II, of which scheme the Mall is the only recognizable remaining feature. It is today one of the most perfect examples of Regency landscaping and planting (work of Nash, 1828). It is unspoilt except for the rhododendrons, planted by the Ministry of Works, lining the path you are now walking on. Pause as you come to the charming little suspension bridge. Raise your camera to the left for an exposure of " Buck House," wind on and expose again for London's most-romantic-view-of-all, pinnacles of Whitehall Court over and behind War Office and Horse Guards Parade. From the bridge you will be able to see the only place of refreshment in the Park. It is called the Cake House. Also in the Park is a weather bulletin board where daily reports are posted for the benefit of the public.

bird life

Use your binoculars to spot two pelicans, Peter (the pink one), and Paul, whose predecessors have been here since and before Evelyn saw them on February 9th, 1665 (recorded in his diary); the first brace were given to Charles II by the Russian Ambassador. They are fed by Mr. Hinton, with fresh herrings, at 4.0 every day. Two swans are also resident; any others present will have flown in from the Thames, and on December 9, 1950, there were 36 varieties of wildfowl on the lake. Beside the Mall, in the distance is the " Citadel " mystery building, extension to the Admiralty built during the war (not a film set for a new frontier fort). Beyond, Waterloo steps designed by the great Townscaper, Nash, to whom we owe Carlton House Terrace (on your right or left) and York column (commemorating George IV's brother, the Duke of York, " put up there to be out of reach of his creditors "), one of London's greatest pieces of sustained monumental town-planning and one of the nicest layouts in Europe. Bomb-damaged and threatened with " rebuilding ", it was taken over by the Government for preservation, who, believe it or not, then threatened to rebuild it themselves.

St. James's

Don't forget you are still on the suspension bridge. From here, if you know how, you can walk through the courtyards of St. James's Palace to Pall Mall, which provides a pleasant reminder of the old tradition of personal contact between subject and Monarch. Turn left, along the lake, bear first right and out into the Mall and enter St. James's Palace by Clarence Gate. Junior not allowed to ride his tricycle, past top-hatted gate keeper and bearskin-topped sentry (who won't take any notice of you). Right, Clarence House (residence in any Royal house is always indicated by the flying of the Royal Standard). Walk up the cobbles into Stable Yard (red-bricked, Georgian and charming). There's a way through to Green Park on the left, but turn right, into Ambassador's Court, and cut under the archway at the end into Pall Mall. Here guiding becomes difficult. First take a peep at Marlborough House, Queen Mary's home, and along its garden wall a statue of Queen Alexandra. Next cross Pall Mall and first passage on the left is Crown Passage. Charming little shopping centre (and if this walk has taken longer than you thought, try the lunch at the Red Lion). You are now at the back of Nos. 3 and 6, Berry's and Lock's (we've already told you about them).

At No. 3 is the entrance to Pickering Place. The right hand wall of the passage is Elizabethan and is half-timbered. Pickering Place was the last duelling ground in London. In it you will find a sundial in the form of an astrolabe, and the head of Lord Palmerston (part of a tombstone). If you peep in at the entrance of No. 4 you will find some interesting prints, one of St. James's as it might have been and one as it was, and charters to hold markets in St. James's. It's worth your while to make a detour down St. James's Place, to see if you can catch the tail end of an auction at Christie's. (No. 27.) Auctions start at 11.0 and last until about 1.30, but you can go in any time.

1 pm

WHERE TO EAT

What's the difference between lunch and dinner? Mrs. Beeton might tell you, but at most restaurants, except for the price, there is little or none. We have split a few hairs and collared a few places which we think are better for lunch—City taverns (not open for meals at night), places with a view (worth seeing by daylight) and cheap spots (we think you might want to save your money for the evening meal). Here it might be worth noting that if you are in a watch-pawning mood (see 9 a.m.) there are the great popular chain-restaurants of Lyons', A.B.C., Express Dairy, where you can probably eat more for less than anywhere else in the world. This guide ignores such honoured Institutions just as it ignores the Department Stores, because they are Institutions which you ought to know already, and our job is to tell you what you might not know. And then there are the old-faithfuls at the other end of the food ladder, Berkeley, Connaught, Ritz, Savoy, Claridge's. It goes without saying that you can feed or stay in them at almost any hour of the day or night, together, according to legend, with (at the Ritz) Diplomats and International Mystery Men, (at Claridge's) Kings crowned and uncrowned, (at the Savoy) Femmes Fatales and the International Spy Ring, (at the Berkeley) " The County " and " The Cavalry " and (at the Connaught) those who regard even decorations and titles as marks of the parvenu.

ROOM WITH A VIEW

HYDE PARK HOTEL Knightsbridge, S.W.1 SLO: 4567	Not quite so central but the restaurant does make contact with Hyde Park and if you're lucky enough to get a window table you will overlook lawns and trees, not to mention flowers, birds and equestriennes. The Knightsbridge district by the way has some very ritzy pubs opposite the Knightsbridge barracks (Household Cavalry barracks) such for instance as The Trevor Arms (lunch can be got here).
MIRABELLE 57, Curzon Street, W.1 GRO: 1940	IF IT'S HOT and you want something right out of doors, remember the courtyard here where you will lunch al fresco under a roof of creepers which might be vine leaves. Very replenishing, as is the highly decorative cold table. Large wine list seems to have some vintages earlier than the eternal '47's and 45's.
RITZ Piccadilly, W.1 REG: 8181	The restaurant is still the only really sophisticated piece of " Louis " in the eating world (Mewes and Davis, architects) and very reviving after all that jazz-modern which *is* jazz and *isn't* modern. A table by the window on a sunny day has a champagne-like quality very rare in these times. Odd thing is that unlike some of Soho the Ritz (except for its cocktails) isn't wildly expensive. The wine and cider cups should be investigated.
96, PICCADILLY W.1 MAY: 9661	Very pleasant too can be a table by the window in the restaurant (as opposed to the grill room) which also overlooks the Green Park, but with scarlet buses in between. Décor here is stage-designer's wedding cake rococo, pink to off-white, nice for those who like that sort of thing. Food as good as the view.
DERRY & TOMS High Street, Kensington, W.8 WES: 8181	Try the roof garden restaurant, not so expensive, but al fresco. Light lunches in the surprisingly large Woodland Garden. Also the Spanish Garden and Tudor Garden (see what London's atmosphere does to flowers). A stream with sheldrakes (ducks to you) a waterfall, fruit trees (the chairmen get the fruit) and a view of London. The 1s. you pay to get on the roof goes to the Hospital Benevolent Fund so don't feel too badly about it.

SEA FOOD, BUTTERIES AND BARS

SHEEKEY'S FISH RESTAURANT 29, St. Martin's Court, Charing Cross Road, W.C.1 TEM: 4118	Started by Mrs. Sheekey in 1896, now run by her daughter, Mrs. Williams. Stage doors of Wyndham's and the New opposite. Frequented by stage people (Basil Radford, Bobby Howes, Michael Redgrave, etc.), many of whose signed photographs adorn the walls. Small marble-topped oyster (12s. a doz.) bar ; two small rooms crowded with tables. A modest 1s. 6d. during the Twenties, your plate of stewed eel or steamed halibut will now cost you 5s. 6d. Open from 12.0 to 8.0. Fully licensed.
DRIVER'S 46, Glasshouse Street, W.1 REG: 4646	Oyster bar, etc. Emphasis on fish food. Suitable for tourists.
BENTLEY'S BAR 15, Swallow Street, W.1 REG: 0431	Emphasis on fish food. Suitable for tourists.

THE HOUSE OF HAMBURGER 1, Leicester Street, W.C.2 GER: 4864	You can get a hamburger (served with a salad at 3s. 6d.) but in spite of its name, this is a fish restaurant. Sit at one of the small tables, or on a stool at the L-shaped bar (chromium glass rails overhead hung with imitation loaves and lobsters) to eat your Whitstable oyster, jellied eel, lobster, or any other kind of fish you fancy. Fully licensed. Open from 12 noon to 12 midnight.
CUNNINGHAM'S 51, Curzon Street, W.1 GRO: 3141	Ultra Fortnum & Mason style with ground floor bar and first floor drawing-room bar-restaurant, damask-chaired, champagne-cocktailed, confidential. Your opulent American relatives will gladly pay 15s. for the speciality, Lobster Cunningham, and 8s. 6d. for other sea food dishes. Awe-inspiring helpings. Wine not the equal of the food.
PRUNIER'S 72, St. James's Street, S.W.1 REG: 1373	Sea foods. A complete importation from Paris.
THE MERMAIDEN Clarges Street, W.1 GRO: 2964	Of the buttery variety is Manetta's sea-food bar The Mermaiden, where for 5s. you can get a delicious truite meunière and when we say delicious we mean it. Your waiter will probably be wearing his waders. This by the way is London home of Swiss wines. Try the Montibeux, white and rather sweet, but not without character. Décor is orthodox moderne but the floor is on a hill which makes for gaiety. Remarkably good white, red and rosé wines (not Swiss) from 5s. a quarter carafe, make for gaiety too. Black Velvet 6s., Coupe de Champagne 6s.
BERKELEY BUTTERY 77, Piccadilly, W.1 REG: 8282	Theoretically this is where you pop in for a snack when you haven't time for a full dress luncheon in the restaurant. Actually, snack luncheons tend to go on longer, work out no cheaper, than the other kind—particularly here where the climate is so bracing. Company chic, cocktails excellent, conversations loud, assured, the accent of privilege.
CLARIDGE'S CAUSERIE Brook Street, W.1 MAY: 8860	It seems more informal than it is. Noted for hors d'œuvres.
FORTNUM & MASON'S 181, Piccadilly, W.1 REG: 8040	Also of the buttery type. Fortnum and Mason's food-lounge, much frequented by the fashionable ladies doing their shopping. Very rich cakes. Don't step on the French poodle.

CITY CHOP HOUSES

PIMM'S 3, Poultry, E.C.2 CIT: 4840	Sandwich bar in old-fashioned pub atmosphere. Patronized by city gents. Stand against the counter with your plate full and a pint. Famous gin-sling with a flower of the herb borage on top and much else underneath, known world-over as a "Pimms," issued from here eighty years ago.
SIMPSON'S 100, Strand, W.C.2 TEM: 7131	The classic house (known the world over) of the Cut From The Joint. Thus uniquely and essentially English. A school of thought holds that Simpson's grow their own bullocks and muttons, for no other meat is comparable. If the chef carves for you, give him a memento of friendship. Try to eat downstairs. Not strictly the City of course, next door to the Savoy.

SIMPSON'S TAVERN Ball Court, 38½, Cornhill, E.C.3 MAN: 8901	We suggest the grill room on the ground floor, where Ernie (been there 45 years) will show you to your seat and hover anxiously over you. Panelled room, high-backed horse boxes, three aside. Speedy service and 6s. will cover you on a three-course lunch. The people you will see, in city suits, with Oxford accents, 90 per cent. male. In a corner of the room, a grill, the coke still glows (to keep the gravy warm). No chops, no steaks. Would you mind putting your hat on the Brass Hat rail Sir? Albert in chef's hat presides over the grill.
DR. BUTLER'S HEAD RESTAURANT Coleman Street, E.C.2 MON: 3504	A.L.C. only and your bill may be 10s. Bar and buffet ground floor. Side entrance to restaurant on the first floor, with a balcony overlooking at second floor level. Half-timbered interior, carpeted floor. Rolls and butter waiting for you, beer obtained from downstairs. Coffee at 6d. comes by the pot. Served by Len, get him to tell you about Dick Turpin. Don't sit waiting to pay the bill—cash desk downstairs.
WATLING RESTAURANT Corner Watling Street and Bow Lane, E.C.4 CIT: 6225	Claims to be the oldest house, first to be built after the Great Fire in the Cordwainers Ward. Reputedly a refreshment house for Wren's workmen. Scheduled as ancient monument. Home from home for Australians during the war. One bar and seats for 20 in the front room (the most picturesque), with hand-cut beams, Hogarth prints and a complete set of proper copper pots. Don't ring the bell unless you want to buy drinks all round.
CHESHIRE CHEESE Wine Office Court, 145, Fleet Street, E.C.4 CEN: 9129	Built 1667 (and they don't let you forget it, it's on all the mustard and pepper pots). Dining room ground floor on the left. Ye fare will probably add up to 10s. Tailed waiters tread the saw-dust floor. Clay pipes in pots line the window sills. Pre-war eminent visitors were given a pipe and tobacco free, but times are changed. Seating mostly in horse boxes, three aside, others on Windsor chairs. Alleged spiritual home of Dr. Johnson.
COCK TAVERN 22, Fleet Street, E.C.4 CEN: 8570	Ground floor, large bar, cast iron columns, barrels; first floor grill room and place to aim for after your pint, for lunch in horse boxes. The original tavern, then The Cock and Bottle, was on the north side of Fleet Street till 1887. Known to Pepys, Thackeray, Dickens and Tennyson, who wrote a poem about it. LOOK OUT FOR original cock sign carved by Grinling Gibbons, kept in the bar out of reach of souvenir hunters.
GEORGE AND VULTURE 3, Castle Court, E.C.3 MAN: 2839	By name one of the oldest taverns in the City. Chaucer would have told you how to get to it—in those days it was called the *George*. Its present name probably derives from its amalgamation with the *Live Vulture* after the Great Fire. Named as Pickwick's London headquarters, although it will probably be more easily found, not by asking for the address, but for St. Michael's Alley, Cornhill. Still a meeting place for the City Pickwick Club. Glass doors are inscribed *Thomas's Chop House*, and chop house it is, with horse boxes and cast iron pillars. The food is good. Have a drink at the bar on the ground floor, but eat upstairs for atmosphere and more speedy service.
HOOP AND GRAPES 47, Aldgate High Street, E.C.3 ROY: 1375	Originally a coaching station at the City's eastern Gate—close by the River at the Tower—it has withstood all the onslaughts of modernisation. With mahogany, chocolate and cream glossy paint, beams, barrels and boarding it retains its character of a port—or riverside—eating pub. Tradition unimpaired and uncommercialised, hard-to-find and unobtrusive; it sits in its little paved recess off the assertive commercialism of the High Street—just as Dr. Johnson may have known it. The Lunch Room—beyond the bar—filled with City men, provides a good setting and a reasonably-priced meal (soup is only 2d.). Landlord, Mr. Saunders, is ready to show visitors around the building.

EASY ON THE PURSE

THE "57" 57, Fetter Lane, E.C.4 CEN: 6953	Near St. Bartholomew-the-Great, the Central Criminal Court, Farringdon Street, or Hatton Garden. Try lunch at the "57" for a nice juicy steak at 4s. (with chips and fried onions of course). First to whet your appetite, prop up the bar of the Shamrock next door, where we can recommend the draught stout. Take your drink with you to the "57," it's permitted. Waiters in white, you in a horse box, your coat in the soup (it's crowded). Finish with cheese and biscuits, unless you prefer *that* type of custard.
THE NEW COSY CAFÉ AND RESTAURANT 54, Little Britain, E.C.1 MON: 9623	London's most crowded café, a Pepsi-Cola outpost, cream and green again, wipe your own table, pass the old cups back, and above the sonorous voice describing a test match, or reading the news, order roast beef, goes down as "Roast and two," "Bread and the best" (bread and butter). Your very satisfying meal, only 2s. 6d., eaten amongst cut-up loaves, a tray of buns (for tea), a milk churn and the most varied collection of people, including medical students from Bart's close by. If not your cup of tea, try the Bartholomew, not quite next door, safe at twice the price.
NEW SCALA RESTAURANT 69, Charlotte Street, W.1 MUS: 6200	Opposite the Scala theatre. Typical real life restaurant, green and cream decorations, steamed-up windows, Coca Cola and foreign film advertisements, Balkan waiters, sish kebab, spaghetti, mixed grill or just plain fish and chips. Ask for bread and you get the best part of a French loaf, ask for your meal and the order is shouted down a lift shaft, ask for coffee and it is drawn from a silver monster next to the cash till. You're covered with about 5s. in your pocket. You will find Toni, the proprietor, down the street at 92, a rather more intimate joint (dare we say low dive?).
STAGE DOOR GRILL 11, (Lower) Wardour Street, W.1 GER: 3583	Central and cheap. Their 3s. TDH (a good 5s. worth) includes ravioli, venison, vol-au-vent, pastries, baklava, and many other items from current and varied menu. Décor includes señoritas, two "Monarchs of the Glen," a tapestry, too big for the proprietor's home, and liberal gold and pink paint, mirrors.
TORINO 61, Dean Street, W.1	One place where you can order minestrone or spaghetti (both if rich) and having paid walk out without comment. Both dishes delicious. Next to you a Briton in boiler suit reading *Daily Mirror*, a Spaniard in leather jerkin and beret, a Frenchman and eight Italians—round a table for four, talking twenty to the dozen. Pink tile table tops and check table cloths, Luigi de Rossi at the cash till. Don't bother to take your coat off. Don't lift the net curtain. Bill about 2s. 9d.
T. WALL & SONS 113, Jermyn Street, W.1 WHI: 1576	(Meat pies and ice cream manufacturers.) Club-like, bowler-hatted atmosphere, determination needed, but as your meal won't come to more than 3s., worth it. Eat at bar, meat pie sales counter at your back, or on high stools up against tableclothed trestle table. *De rigueur* are sausages and pie de jour (their own); optional: soup, milk, salad, cake.
THE WESTMINSTER TECHNICAL COLLEGE 76, Vincent Square, S.W.1 VIC: 4221	"Lunch, Sir? At a modest price, Sir? Certainly, Sir. Will 3s. be too much, Sir?" What do you get for 3s.? Why, you might easily get smoked salmon, chicken, apricot pie and coffee. Where is this wonderful place? (The restaurant with the ever so faintly unprofessional atmosphere.) You will be having lunch at a school for waiters (2 year course in hotel operation run by the Westminster Technical Institute, to be exact). The hotel manager to be, who is serving you, might have had a hand in the preparation of your meal and will be back in the classroom at 2.0. Be there at 12.30.

2 pm

ON VIEW

This section is about as close as you will ever come to a guide book. Museums and art exhibitions in this list are the decidedly more unusual ones, of which there are quite a number, lurking in side streets and slightly out-of-town districts.

These should show you something more of the British collector's instinct than you normally would see.

MUSEUMS

You will have no trouble finding the Crown Jewels and the Armoury in the Tower of London, or the British Museum in Great Russell Street (antiquities, ethnography, and books, 10-5.30, Sundays, 2.30-6). The rest of the high-museum stuff is in the Kensington area, housed in some of the most horrific buildings our island race has produced:—The Victoria and Albert Museum (ornamental and decorative art, 10-6, Sundays, 2.30-6), the Imperial Institute (life and resources of the Empire, 10-4.30 weekdays only), the Natural History and Science Museums (10-6, Sundays 2.30-6). We are listing the smaller or lesser known museums, collections and exhibitions.

STERLINGS, CAXTONS, SUGGS, CAMBERWELLS. Butterflies? Printers' type? No—the names of street lamps. The most comprehensive display in the country, including part of Peter Varnon's private collection, and the late Dean Chandler's collection of antique interior and exterior gas fittings, can be seen at William Sugg, Ranelagh Works, Chapter Street, S.W.1, Ring VIC: 3211 before visiting.

FOR THE NAUTICAL, over forty merchant ship figure-heads as well as much other maritime matter is on show just outside London at Captain L. J. Silver's very astonishing nautical museum, The Lookout, Waterfront, Gravesend, Kent (Gravesend 1176, town number, AMB: 1767). Please call the cleaner stewardess, the janitor bo'sun, and Mrs. Silver the mate. Likewise, lounge is the poop, bedroom the cabin, kitchen the galley. Hand-tinted pictures of the last century in seashell frames. Signal flags over lavatory door read: "I can hold out no longer" and the flags inside: "I have ——", but then why don't you ask?

ARE YOU A SPECIALIST? You will be able to study your favourite subject in the Parkes Museum, at 90, Buckingham Palace Road, S.W.1. A long line of white and blue iris patterned W.C.'s including every tortured type invented from 1870 up to today. Don't miss the brilliantly coloured art nouveau tiled panels which attempt to cheer this gaunt and fusty room. Open, free, daily, 10–5; Saturdays 10–12.30.

LONDON MUSEUM, opening in June. Very well worth while, with corny but effective dioramas, Landing of Claudius, Fire of London, etc., and some very good early plans and models of the city. London's history made as plain as a pikestaff here at Kensington Palace, centre of much of it—speaking of history, it was at Kensington Palace that Victoria came downstairs in her nightie, in the same building as this museum, to be acclaimed Queen of England.

SIR JOHN SOANE'S HOUSE (which is now his museum), 13, Lincoln's Inn Fields, W.C.2. This of course you will have visited anyway, but go again to admire the romantic taste of this classic architect who is immensely honoured today by all but the governors of the Bank of England who mutilated his masterpiece in order to house a few more functionaries.

MUSEUM OF THE CORPORATION OF THE CITY OF LONDON. In charge of a library attendant but, if you really want the low down, ask to see Mr. Cook, the keeper. Exhibits; mostly mediaeval articles including horse-shoes, woollen caps, spurs, shears, ornaments, games and toys, money, keys, tiles, weapons, sculpture, seals, and books.

IN SAME BUILDING alongside perpendicular Gothic of Sir Horace Jones's 1873 Guildhall library is a little room lined and hung with cased-in clocks and watches. Most delicate of all are the jewelled watch keys; most dynamic, the rising brass spiral of the Italian hydrogen gas clock. This, the Clockmakers' Company Museum, Guildhall, E.C.2, is supposed to be the most complete collection in the country. Admittance, free. Hours: 10–5.

THERE IS MUCH TO BE LEARNT at the Building Centre, 9, Conduit Street, W.1 (shortly to move to 26, Store Street). It is a museum of modern building methods and equipment, the most elaborate existing display of the bits and pieces which go to make up the buildings in which you live and work, the structural elements, the fittings for bathroom and kitchen, gas

fires, heaters, materials. And it tells you where to get them. This centre, the first of its kind, was created by its present Director, F. R. Yerbury, a figure of international renown in the building world. It has been the model on which have been based other building centres throughout the world.

FOR MILITARY HISTORY, the United Services Museum, in Inigo Jones's Banqueting Hall in Whitehall, where Charles I was beheaded. Leave the children studying the model battles, and spare a moment to look at the recently cleaned painting on the ceiling above, of the Apotheosis of James I, by Rubens. If you want to know what missed you in the last war (flying bombs and V.2's) and a comprehensive display of the means by which you hit back, go to the Imperial War Museum, Lambeth Road, S.E.1. Hours, 10–6, Sundays 2–6; admission free.

WELLINGTON MUSEUM, Apsley House, built of red brick, 1771–8, by the Adam brothers. Faced with stone and a Corinthian portico, 1828–9. The Duke of Wellington went to live there in 1816. Left to the nation by the 7th Duke in 1947 to display works of art, personal possessions and relics of the Iron Duke. To be administered by the V. & A. Museum and opened as soon as possible. 149, Piccadilly, W.1 (perhaps better known as No. 1, London).

COURTAULD INSTITUTE OF ART. Town house by Robert Adam, built for Lord Home, 1771–8. Now belonging to the University of London. When you go, look out for ballroom, drawing room, music room, Chinese room and twin-flight staircase joining at the intermediate landing, round a circular well with dome-shaped skylight. 19, Portman Square, W.1. Admission 10-1, Saturdays.

DR. JOHNSON lived in a sunny corner of Gough Square (No. 17) for 11 years, from 1748 to 59. Of his own furniture only two chairs and a walking stick remain. The armchair has quite recovered from the strain of bearing his great weight, and polish, dusters, new carpets and time have quite removed the smell of him. But you are at liberty to visit what remains of him here. Mrs. Rowell, full of Johnsoniana as a feminine Boswell could be, will tell you of the three copyists working incessantly in the garret, and of the pine panelling brought from America. Hours : 10.30-5. Admission 1s.

DICKENS MUSEUM AND LIBRARY. Cream and brown, and shiny linoleum, sketches, "jolly" cartoons and original manuscripts : an author's house, but inhabited mostly by his characters. To be found at 48, Doughty Street, W.C.1. Open 10-12.30 and 2-5 except Sundays. Admission, 1s.

CARLYLE'S HOUSE is brown and sombre. Wood panelling, painted graining, Morris wallpapers, early Victorian furniture and delicate balustrading on a Queen Anne staircase. Before you leave, call on Henrietta Strong in her kitchen in the basement. Here the house comes to life again as she describes how she and her mother have, for the last 56 years, looked after Mr. and Mrs. Carlyle's effects as though they were still living. One flaw : the ground floor rooms, once inter-communicating, as shown in Robert Tait's painting of the Carlyles, are now separate, as the backroom is occupied by the housekeeper. The front room, however (the one in which Jenny kissed me), is almost exactly as it was. At 24, Cheyne Row, S.W.3. Hours, 10-6 in summer, 10 to dusk in winter. Admission, 1s., Saturdays 6d.

ART EXHIBITIONS

Antique Masters to the present day. All periods represented, but for most part contemporary, with particular emphasis on British art over the last century.

Some of the more interesting are : RENOIR, Marlborough Fine Art Ltd., 18, Old Bond Street, W.1, until May 12 ; ROYAL SOCIETY OF PAINTERS IN WATERCOLOURS, SPRING EXHIBITION, R.W.S. Gallery, 26, Conduit Street, W.1, until May 31 ; EAST LONDON IN 1851, AND BRITISH POPULAR ART, Whitechapel Art Gallery, E.1, until June 29 ; CONTEMPORARY BRITISH PAINTING (1925-1950), New Burlington Galleries, 3, Burlington Gardens, W.1, until mid-June ; WORKS BY MICHAEL AYRTON, UTRILLO, ADRIAN RYAN, CHRISTOPHER WOOD, Redfern Gallery, 20, Cork Street, W.1, until June 29 ; WORKS BY THOMAS LAWRENCE, Agnew's, 43, Old Bond Street, W.1, until June 29 ; THE ENGLISH SCENE. IMPORTANT PAINTINGS OF THREE CENTURIES, Roland, Browse & Delbanco, 19, Cork Street, W.1, until June 16 ; HENRY MOORE. ARTS COUNCIL EXHIBITION, Tate Gallery, S.W.1, until July 29 ; RETROSPECTIVE EXHIBITION OF THE WORK OF THE R.S.A. (1851-1951), R.S.A. Gallery, 6, John Adam Street, W.C.2, until Oct. 31 ; LEADING CHARACTERS OF 1851, National Portrait Gallery, St. Martin's Lane, W.C.2, May 4-Sept. 30 ; TRADITIONAL ART FROM THE COLONIES, Imperial Institute, Exhibition Road, S.W.7, May 4-Sept. 30 ; ROYAL ACADEMY SUMMER EXHIBITION, Burlington House, W.1, May 5-Aug. 12 ; UTRILLO, Marlborough Fine Art Ltd., 18, Old Bond Street, W.1, May 15-June 2 ; ROYAL SOCIETY OF BRITISH ARTISTS FESTIVAL EXHIBITION, R.B.A. Galleries, Suffolk Street, S.W.1, May 21-June 14 ; ART IN THE SERVICE OF THE CHURCH (An Exhibition of contemporary design and craftmanship), Lambeth Palace, June 4-Aug. 31 ; RECENT PAINTINGS BY GRAHAM SUTHERLAND, Hanover Gallery, 32a, St. George Street, W.1, June 12 to end of summer ; TEMPERA PAINTINGS BY WILLIAM BLAKE, Arts Council Gallery, 4, St. James's Square, S.W.1, June 16-July 14 ; CONTEMPORARY BRITISH PAINTING (1925-1950), New Burlington Galleries, W.1, June 19-July 28 ; SIXTY PAINTINGS FOR 1951—BY INVITATION OF THE ARTS COUNCIL, R.B.A. Galleries, Suffolk Street, S.W.1, June 20-July 31 ; HOGARTH : ARTS COUNCIL EXHIBITION, Tate Gallery, S.W.1, June 29-July 29 ; BRITAIN (1921-1951) LONDON OCCASIONS, LONDON CEREMONIES, AND PERSONALITIES, Guildhall Art Gallery, E.C.4, July 2-Aug. 31 ; NATIONAL EXHIBITION OF CHILDREN'S ART, Royal Institute Galleries, 195, Piccadilly, W.1, Sept. 6-Sept. 28 ; ROYAL INSTITUTE OF OIL PAINTERS EXHIBITION, Royal Institute Galleries, W.1, Oct. 16-Nov. 7 ; ROYAL SOCIETY OF PAINTERS IN WATERCOLOURS : AUTUMN EXHIBITION and ROYAL MINIATURE SOCIETY, R.W.S. Gallery, 26, Conduit Street, W.1, Nov. 2-Dec. 5 ; ROYAL SOCIETY OF PORTRAIT PAINTERS EXHIBITION, Royal Institute Galleries, W.1, Nov. 20-Dec. 29.

3 pm
YOUR GAME

We don't dare claim that sport in London is better than elsewhere, but there's certainly a lot of it. Cricket, football, ice-hockey, skating, greyhound, speedway and horse-racing, to list just a few categories. And in another category (the sports that you can take part in) are boating, sailing, riding, golf. For current information: the list of sporting events every day in *The Times*, 3d., or on Friday (covering week ahead) *What's On in London*, 6d.

cricket
Principal London grounds are: Lord's, St. John's Wood, belonging to the Marylebone Cricket Club (the M.C.C.), the Middlesex C.C. also play here; Thomas Lord (of Lord's) moved his cricket field twice before it came to rest. It started as a hired field in what is now Dorset Square. It was moved to St. John's Wood (he took the turf with him the first move) in 1812. The Oval (Kennington), headquarters of the Surrey C.C. These are the two grounds for first-class cricket. Much other cricket to be found in London—some of the most pleasant to watch being that played in traditional surroundings on one-time village greens such as: Kew Green, Ham Common, Giggshill Green (nr. Kingston), Richmond Green, Mitcham Green and Chiswick Park. (Information—*Wisden's Cricketers' Almanack*, Sporting Handbooks, Ltd., 10s. 6d. and 12s. 6d.)

golf
One point to note—generally speaking best sandy soils for golf predominate roughly from south to west of London. Immediately north is a belt of clay—dry in summer but wet in winter (many good clubs, however, do exist to north). Many courses round London (over 260 within 50 miles). Public and municipal ones (with low green fees) at: Richmond Park; Beckenham Place Park, Kent; Whitewebbs,

Enfield, Middlesex; Addington Court, Surrey; Haste Hill, Middlesex; Rickmansworth, Herts; Brent Valley, Hanwell, Middlesex; Hainault Forest, Essex; Royal Epping Forest, Chingford; Coulsdon Court, Surrey. Crowded at week-ends. Visitors welcomed at practically all private clubs on week-days. Advisable to contact secretary in advance (particularly for week-end play). No play week-ends for unintroduced non-members (particularly ladies) at some clubs. Among many near ones to London (all 18 holes):—

SOUTH EAST. Sundridge Park, Bromley, Kent (RAVensbourne 0278); 11 miles—very pleasant. Royal Blackheath, Eltham, S.E.9 (ELTham 1042)—11 miles—oldest club in England, founded 1608; clubhouse has many golf treasures. Knole Park, Sevenoaks, Kent (Sevenoaks 2150)—28 miles—best park course near London according to Henry Longhurst (near Sackvilles' fine house).

SOUTH. Malden, New Malden, Surrey (MALden 0654)—9 miles. Addington, Shirley Church Road, Surrey (Springpark 1300)—12 miles—first class. Addington Palace, Addington Park, Addington (ADDiscombe 3061)—12 miles—clubhouse formerly residence of the Archbishop of Canterbury. Purley Downs, Purley, Surrey (Sanderstead 1231)—14 miles. Selsdon Park, Sanderstead, Surrey (Sanderstead 3127)—15 miles—good hotel accommodation. Cuddington, Banstead, Surrey (Ewell 1891-2)—15 miles. Tandridge, Oxted, Surrey (Oxted 573-4)—23 miles.

SOUTH-WEST. Royal Wimbledon, Wimbledon Common, S.W.19 (WIMbledon 0055)—8 miles—first class (introduction essential). Royal Mid-Surrey, Richmond, Surrey (RIChmond 1894)—8 miles—2 courses; flat but first-class; professional, Henry Cotton. Richmond, Sudbrook Park, Surrey (RIChmond 1463)—9 miles—1726 club house designed by James Gibbs. Coombe Hill, Surrey (KINgston 5183)—10 miles—(introduction essential). Fulwell, Hampton Hill, Middlesex (Molesey 188)—12 miles (near Hampton Court). Burhill, Walton-on-Thames, Surrey (Walton 2345)—19 miles—good, sandy, woods and heather (with a historic mansion, the King's House). R.A.C. Country Club, Epsom, Surrey (Ashstead 666)—16 miles—also tennis, swimming, etc. (open to members of foreign A.C.'s associated with R.A.C.). St. George's Hill, Weybridge, Surrey (Weybridge 406)—20½ miles—first class. Woking, Surrey (Woking 453)—28 miles—one of the best courses in Surrey. West Hill, Brookwood, Surrey (Brookwood 3266)—33 miles—another first grade course.

WEST. Ealing, Greenford, Middlesex (PERivale 2595)—7 miles. Stanmore, Middlesex (Grims Dyke 287)—14 miles. Stoke Poges, near Slough, Bucks (Slough 23321)—20 miles. Berkshire, Ascot, Berks (Ascot 549)—29 miles—heath land, two excellent courses. Camberley Heath, Camberley, Surrey (Camberley 258)—32 miles—very picturesque. Temple, near Maidenhead, Berks (Hurley 248)—31 miles—some of finest views in England.

NORTH. Hendon, Holders Hill, Hendon, N.W.4 (HENdon 1008)—8 miles. Finchley, Nether Court, N.W.7 (FINchley 2436)—9 miles—old clubhouse. Mill Hill, 100, Barnet Way, Mill Hill (MILl Hill 2282)—11 miles—interesting. South Herts, Totteridge, N.20 (HILlside 0017)—11 miles—Dai Rees succeeded Vardon as professional. Old Fold Manor. Hadley Green, Barnet, Herts (BARnet 2266)—13 miles. Hadley Wood, near Barnet, Herts (BARnet 4486)—14 miles—good. Sandy Lodge, Northwood, Herts (Northwood 129)—16 miles—sandy and first class; Vardon helped design it. Northwood, Middlesex (Northwood 29)—16 miles. West Herts, Cassiobury Park, Watford (Watford 4264)—18 miles—one of few sandy N. courses. Berkhamsted, Herts (Berkhamsted 555)—28 miles—fine example of old fashioned common course, natural hazards. Ashridge, Little Gaddesden, Herts (Little Gaddesden 2244)—31 miles—Cotton formerly professional; excellent "forest" course, fine fairways.

Also worth noting are these first-class courses laid out, amid fine scenery, with everything money and brains could devise: Walton Heath, Tadworth, Surrey (Tadworth 2060)—18 miles. Sunningdale, Surrey (Ascot 681)—24 miles. Wentworth, Virginia Water, Surrey (Wentworth 2201)—22 miles. Worplesdon, Woking, Surrey (Brookwood 2277)—34 miles. Moor Park, Rickmansworth, Herts (Rickmansworth 1346)

—17 miles—famous clubhouse designed by Giacomo Leoni in 1720. (For information see *The Golfer's Handbook*, 20s.; feature " Where to Golf " in *Golf Illustrated*, Wednesday, 1s.)

greyhound racing
Tracks are at: Catford, Charlton, Clapton, Hackney Wick, Harringay, Hendon, New Cross, Stamford Bridge, Park Royal, Wandsworth, Wembley (fairest graded track in the country, races Mondays and Saturdays), West Ham, White City, Wimbledon. (For fixtures see the *Greyhound Express*, daily, 2d.; *The Sporting Life*, daily, 3d., and the ordinary dailies.)

motor boating
Motor boats for the week, or longer, can be obtained from many points on the Thames. Firms at Kingston, Hampton Court, Sunbury, Walton, Shepperton, Weybridge and other places. Prices vary according to season and size. During May to June and September to October costs range from about £17,10s. to £30 per week, for 4- or 6-berth cruisers. July and August prices rise to £20 to £35. If available, craft can be hired for week-ends (at about half the weekly charge). You can go above Lechlade (only a few miles below the source of the Thames) and down to the sea. If not drawing too much water you can explore parts of the tributaries of the Thames, and the canals. (See advertisements in *The Yachting World*, monthly, 2s., and the *Motor Boat and Yachting*, monthly, 2s.)

racing
The London race-courses are: Alexandra Park, N.22; Sandown Park, Esher, Surrey; Kempton Park, Sunbury, Middlesex; Hurst Park, Molesey, Surrey; Epsom, Surrey (the City and Suburban in April, the Derby and the Oaks in June). Within easy reach of London are: Windsor; Lingfield Park, Surrey; Ascot, Berks (Ascot week in June); Goodwood (at the end of July); Fontwell Park; Brighton; Lewes; Plumpton (last five all in Sussex). The flat-race season is from March to November; steeplechasing goes on throughout the year except for June, July and most of August. Epsom, Goodwood, Brighton, Lewes and Alexandra Park have only flat-races; Plumpton and Fontwell Park only jumping meetings. The remainder have both. During almost every week of the year there is a meeting at one or other of these courses. Write to secretaries of courses for fixture lists.

riding
For Rotten Row (Hyde Park) horses can be obtained from various stables, mostly in the neighbourhood of Knightsbridge (average cost 12s. 6d. per hour). Further afield, the nearest open spaces, Richmond (Richmond Park and Wimbledon Common close by). There are stables at Sheen Gate,

Robin Hood Gate (The London School of Equitation), Petersham, Wimbledon and Kingston, etc. Also riding on Streatham Common, and at Hampton Court and Bushey Park (close by). Epsom (15 miles) has many livery stables and is particularly suitable with its downs (and the Derby Course) and open country beyond. To the north, Hampstead Heath. (Useful list of riding schools and stables advertised in *Riding*, monthly, 1s. 3d. The British Horse Society, 66, Sloane Street, S.W.1, will also supply information.)

rowing

Rowing-boats (at about 2s. 6d. per hour), electric canoes, or small motor craft, can be hired on the Thames (Windsor, Maidenhead and Bray) in the non tidal section; also on The Serpentine (Hyde Park) and the lakes (Regent's Park and Battersea Park) where there are ponds for juniors.

sailing

The best sailing around London is on the Thames, and many private clubs exist. Not many sailing craft for hire. Occasionally odd boats, varied in quality and size, are let out. But two places in particular have facilities: Kingston, Hart & Co. (Elmbridge 2113), have a number of excellent 12 to 16 ft. dinghies; Bourne End (about 28 miles by road), Townsend Bros. (Bourne End 113) also have boats for hire. Prices: from about 5s. per hour to £2 per day.

speedway

Motor-cycle (dirt track) racing takes place from Easter until October. Tracks are at Wembley, Harringay, New Cross, Wimbledon and Walthamstow. (For fixtures see the daily papers, various weekly and monthly speedway magazines, and *What's On*.)

4 pm
CUPPA

A grand old English custom, which has become an International ritual, thank goodness, which means that we can get English teas abroad and the whipped-cream type Continental ones at home. Continental teas seem about the best these days,

Viennese coffee with Schlagobers on top, and cheese cakes or Apfelkuchen. We have found a few of these places although the Tea Centre (British to the extent of not serving China tea) may remain your favourite. Or perhaps you don't take tea at all and would be quite happy to see the Chimpanzees try it at the Zoo (any sunny afternoon).

FOR EDUCATION WITH YOUR TEA go to the Tea Centre, 22, Regent Street, S.W.1. WHI: 8632, 10.30 to 6.30. Passing through the entrance hall stop to admire the exhibits; the wall map showing the tea-producing areas of the world, the large diorama of a tea garden in Ceylon and interesting displays of historical prints. The mural on your right is by John Farleigh. Enquire about machines, recent products of this age, which tell you the time, ring an alarm, light up, boil water, make tea (and might be adapted to strip off your bedclothes). Pass into the tea lounge, a world of concealed lighting, soft colours: note the new screen designed by Fry, Drew and Partners. Here (from 3 p.m.) you can get a 2s. tea in seated comfort, or, if in a hurry, try the quick service counter. Nowhere are you permitted to forget tea is something more serious than a drink—notice the tea factory model; notice, too, the particularly attractive china, an added enticement to confirmed tea-drinkers. Memento-collectors can buy twopenny post-card reproductions on their way out, from the lady out front. In the lounge, a choice of Indian, Ceylonese, Indonesian or a blend; at the quick service counter, blended only.

BENDICK'S, BOND STREET. Tiny-table-teeny-stool type with off-white objects in raffia, not cheap, but everything including the cakes and coffee highly edible.

PROSPECTING FOR A RESTAURANT in Soho by peeping through windows? Look in at Maison Bertaux, 28, Greek Street. Open 9.30 to 6.0. Will do equally well for coffee in the morning. For that matter, to your horror maybe, you can have coffee in the afternoon. Salon de Thé au premier, in pink, concealed lighting and gilt mirrors. Seats a very tight 28, with no room for coat hangers. Cakes at 6d. each, a cup of coffee at the same price. Shop and pay desk are on the ground floor. Owned by that excellent firm, De Bry, which has one branch in New Oxford Street, and another one at Marble Arch.

BEEN BUYING BOOKS in the Charing Cross Road? Away with you to round the corner into Old Compton Street. At No. 9 is Georges Jacquet, father and son, Swiss patissiers. Comfortable room for 12. Better known for their coffee than their tea. You can take cakes away at 2s. 6d. a box of about seven. Omelettes at 2s. 6d. or 3s. at any time of day.

WALK A LITTLE BIT FURTHER up towards Oxford Street and look out for 82, Berwick Street on the left hand side. Here at the Patisserie Bruxelloise, you can have coffee or tea. Emil Vandermissen came over in the first world war and you will find him in the bakery at the back of the shop. You can see all that goes on there by looking in the mirror. The counter comes from Italy. Seated comfort for eight.

HAD A STUFFY TIME AT THE MUSEUMS, been round Hyde Park or to the Albert Hall? Before coming back to the West End walk down to the European Patisserie, Thurloe Street, South Kensington. Very inspiring coffee or chocolate, with Schlagobers at 1s., and delicious cakes at 8d. each. Austrian and Hungarian spoken.

IF YOU WANT TO BE SHOWN to your table by a count and want to hear the sound of Danish voices once again; repair to the Wyvex (pronounced Veev-ex) and named after Copenhagen's best known restaurant, at 87, Wigmore Street (WEL: 1969). Count Scheel is manager. Open from 9.30 to 5.30. We like it for tea, coffee out on the pavement (room for six).

YARNERS COFFEE LTD. Two floors to have coffee (a pot at 1s. gives you three cups) or tea (Darjeeling only), cakes and sandwiches of the expensive (Mortadella and Bismarck Herring) variety. Upstairs a number of window tables overlooking the Ship (B.B.C.) and Upper Regent Street. Decorations: pink carpet, cream ceilings and walls, red cloth in places, green woodwork, violent yellow veneer to chairs and tables (glass topped). Green and orange plastic cruets, waitress in black with little pink apron and cap. All this at 1, Langham Place.

5 pm

SPECIAL EVENT

Having had your cup of char, sit back for a while (before trying out a new pub) and make a few notes in your diary of some of the special events of this Festival year. You're sure to find something in London to suit your taste, whether it be ceremony, exhibition, show, festival or sporting event. We only have room here to list a few ceremonies.

CEREMONIES

The British, bless 'em, are supposed to be rather good at putting on the picturesque ceremony. Plenty of opportunities are provided throughout the year for visitors to judge whether this is true. Here are some of them:

CHANGING THE GUARD at the Palace takes place every morning from 10.30-11.30. The Guard is provided by a detachment from one of the regiments stationed at Wellington or Chelsea Barracks, which also provides a band to play in the Palace forecourt during ceremony. Go when the King's in residence (denoted by flying of Royal Standard) and the Guard is at full strength.

MOUNTING THE GUARD at the Horse Guards, Whitehall, daily at 11-11.15 (Sunday 10-10.15); again a better show when the King's in London. Troops ride (two abreast) down from Hyde Park Barracks, via Hyde Park, Hyde Park Corner, Constitution Hill and the Mall to the Horse Guards Parade. Normally commanded by an officer, accompanied by a squadron corporal-major carrying the standard and a trumpeter mounted on a grey horse. Sentries are changed every hour until the Guard is dismounted for inspection at 4 o'clock. Guard is formed (on alternate days) from the two regiments of Household Cavalry; the Life Guards in red tunics, white helmet plumes, white lambskin saddles, and the Royal Horse Guards (The Blues) in dark blue tunics, red plumes and black saddles. The Guard has mounted over the old Palace of Whitehall continuously for two hundred years, except for the 1939-45 war. One of the duties of the sentries is to allow only those people who have the King's permission to drive (you can walk) through the arch; they have to show an ivory pass specially issued for the purpose.

YOU MUSTN'T MISS seeing a State Opening of Parliament. The King and Queen drive there in the glittering Irish State Coach, accompanied by other members of the Royal family and escorted by Yeomen of the Guard and Household Cavalry. Before the opening, Yeomen with lanterns search the build-

ings and notify the King that all is well; a precaution taken ever since Guy Fawkes tried to blow up the House in 1605.

If you find THE LURE OF THE PARADE, the procession and ceremonial occasion irresistible, here are some more for you:— State Visit of King Frederick and Queen Ingrid of Denmark, May 8-11; British Legion Parade at Cenotaph, May 13; Founder's Day Parade at Royal Hospital, Chelsea, May 29; The Royal Tournament, Earl's Court, June 6-23; King's Official Birthday—Trooping of the Colour Ceremony, Horse Guards Parade, June 7; Service to commemorate the Sealing of Magna Carta, Runnymede, Egham, Surrey, July 1; The King and Queen and General Eisenhower to attend service in memory of U.S. Forces who lost their lives in the British Isles during second World War, St. Paul's Cathedral, July 4; Opening of Michaelmas Law Term—special service at Westminster Abbey, Oct. 1; Trafalgar Day Ceremony—Naval Parade at Trafalgar Square, Oct. 21; Lord Mayor's Show—Procession through London, Nov. 9; Remembrance Sunday—Commemoration service at Cenotaph, Nov. 11.

6 pm

PUBS

Many books have been written about pubs*. In a paragraph, all we can do is to invite you to distinguish between the various sorts of pub, the various sorts of bar and the various sorts of beer. If you don't know the local customs of London pubs and want to be sure of asking for the right

* Read BACK TO THE LOCAL by Maurice Gorham and Edward Ardizzone, (Percival Marshall, 8s. 6d.) and INSIDE THE PUB by Maurice Gorham and H. McG. Dunnett, (Architectural Press, 18s.)

kind of drink in the right kind of bar, the following will be useful.

types of bar

Nearly all pubs have at least two bars: the PUBLIC BAR where the beer and decorations are cheapest, and the SALOON BAR, the superior end of the house, where you pay a penny or two more ; you will probably be using the saloon bar although in certain pubs it is " smarter " to use the public bar. In between these two there are mysterious doors marked PRIVATE BAR, which aren't private at all except in the sense that they aren't public—they are in-betweeners, so if you are an in-betweener walk right in. There may also be a JUG-AND-BOTTLE BAR where you can buy bottled beer or have a jug filled with draught beer to take home. All pubs keep several kinds of bottled and draught beers.

the different brews

Bottled beers are easy: *light ale, brown ale, Guinness, Bass, Worthington*, and so on: you order them by the names on the labels and they usually come in half-pint bottles. But the draught kinds are more tricky. If you simply ask for " beer " or " ale," for instance, you will get half a pint of *mild ale*, which is also called " wallop " and is the cheapest and weakest beer and maybe not what you expected. The three main kinds of draught beer are *bitter beer*, pale coloured and generally the strongest ; *mild ale*, a darker, sweeter, cheaper drink; and *Burton* (sometimes called " old "), very dark and sweet and often quite strong. You order them by asking simply for a bitter, a mild or a Burton and you will be given a half-pint. If you want a pint you must say so. The interesting point is the mixtures of these beers: the gent beside you may ask for a *mild-and-bitter*, a *bitter-and-Burton* or an *old-and-mild* (Burton and mild). They are all exactly what they sound like though for some reason a mild-and-bitter always seems to contain more mild than bitter. It's because the mild is cheaper perhaps. In addition to beer, all but pure beer-houses sell sherries and ports (measures, qualities and prices varying from house to house) and spirits, which present no problem: you simply order "singles" (which Maurice Gorham describes as "the smallest amount of drink yet known to man") or "doubles," depending on your thirst.

That, of course, isn't the half of it but it's enough to start you off on the right foot. You'll pick up the rest as you go along. What, for instance, is a *Pig's Ear*, a *Dog's Nose*, a *Drop*, a *Collar*—you'll find out.

pub types

Speaking generally there are three London pub types all with their particular colours—colour is very important in pubs. First, the ALEHOUSE type which follows the functional tradition in its use of solid carpentry, scrubbed wood tables and bar-top, and "grained oak" or "teak" paint. A particularly satisfying sort of pub, this type has an immensely long history, stemming from the middle ages, when any wayside house opening its doors for the sale of liquor would automatically invite the passer-by into the kitchen. It is in fact the kitchen vernacular. Many London pubs and public bars are of this type, or of the type of its younger and slicker town cousin the City Tavern. In the CITY TAVERN, wines and spirits and bottled beers tend to take precedence over beer-in-cask, though there tend to be even more casks

(chocolate or nigger brown now) which will be for port or sherry, rather than beer. The third type is the GIN PALACE, be-mirrored, be-lettered, be-plushed (walls and bar mahogany, either the real wood or paint-grained), the great Victorian contribution to the architecture of drink and as a building type, one of England's most prized possessions. Unfortunately the brewers, who have lost touch with their best traditions, are trying to break up gin palace interiors in the mistaken notion that they represent a vulgar phase in the history of drinking. To kill them, they are putting in jazz wallpapers, chromium bars, and graining that gives the effect of pickled or even of grey-wood panelling, a beastly development of genteelism, which tends to give the pub the semblance of a night-club or road-house, two very inferior institutions. Worse still, in the cause of "supervision" the licensing magistrates are helping on the bad work by demanding that the succession of intimate little bars, which are the pride and pearl of the English pub should be gutted in favour of one large bar. Result—loss of the cosiness and surprise that used to make a pub the favourite meeting place of friends. If you are one of those people who resent such atrocities and are not afraid to say so, you can help in the fight against the genteelising of pubs by speaking out boldly about the decorations to your neighbour over a pint of wallop. If your temperament is more retiring, just do it by choosing to drink in the un-tarted up ones. We aren't suggesting that the pubs we list are all period pieces; but they are some of the best that remain and all still have something of the real pub character. Tourists should bear in mind the anomalies of the system of licensing hours, but it is safe to assume that pubs in and near the West End are open from 11.30 a.m. to

3 p.m. and from 5.30 until 11 p.m., and that others open half an hour later and close at 2.30 and 10.30. Hours on Sunday are shorter.

West End

Categorised for your convenience into two groups. Those within a threepenny bus ride of Piccadilly, mainly Belgravia, Mayfair, Soho and Bloomsbury; and ones further afield.

THE GRENADIER, Wilton Row, S.W.1. Museum example of the mews pub, completely tucked away, veiled for ever from the main-streeters. Once the rendezvous of coachmen, it is now the " local " for the mews village (of extremely expensive houses) that surrounds it. Pub connoisseurs particularly cherish its exterior, as it is an unspoilt example of the ' functional tradition ' (See Intro. and *Spread Eagle and Crown*). This is the kind of pub the brewers are trying to jazz up, as in their perverse way they are trying to genteelise the jazzed-up kind (the Gin Palace).

THE COACH AND HORSES, Kinnerton Street, Belgravia, S.W.1. Another example of mews ale-shop. Small, unobtrusive and intimate. From the hatchway in the little back room at street level you get a see-but-not-seen view of life in the larger bar in the basement. The draught Guinness is excellent.

THE STAR TAVERN, Belgrave Mews West, S.W.1. Next door to the arched north entrance to the mews, you can sit outside on the benches and watch the cobblestones go by. Background music is the jargon of the motor-racing fraternity.

ANTELOPE, Eaton Terrace, S.W.1. Once the Dome and Rotonde of London's Bohemia, featuring Augustus John, Philip Heseltine; now very much the haunt of the lads and lasses of Belgravia, with barmen in white coats and high prices, but lots of style without losing the essential pub atmosphere. Details right; including the lettering and exterior colours which are highly reminiscent of Christopher Wood. You can get a glass of wine there as well as beer. Restaurant attached. Chelsea pensioners frequent public bar.

TREVOR ARMS, Knightsbridge, S.W.1. Soft lights, and carpet. Where Life Guards officers, from the barracks next door, take their girls. No kitchen vernacular about this.

THE ENTERPRISE, Tachbrook Street, Pimlico, S.W.1. Draught Bass. Typical butcher, baker, candlestickmaker London pub. Varnished lincrusta and screwed-down tables. Look out for lettered mirror which was cracked and pock-marked in the bombing. On November 11th poppies are put in all the holes. Inscription below tells you all about it.

HOLE IN THE WALL, Sloane Square Station, Westbound platform (built in 1868). Gains its uniqueness by being on the actual platform, so that you walk out of the train into the pub. The reverse procedure may require rather more care.

THE RED LION, Duke of York Street, St. James's, S.W.1. First-rate specimen of rococo Victorian pub; two tiny bars. Its miniature scale enhances the jewel-like effect of glittering patterned glass, mahogany curlicues and ferns in pots. The barmaids really are twins—not the same one seen again in one of the innumerable mirrors. One of few remaining Gin Palace type.

THE GOAT, Stafford Street (Old Bond Street), W.1. One of the oldest and smallest pubs in the district. Very intimate and simple. Benches, grained oak. Good collection of early play-bills.

SHEPHERD'S, Shepherd Market, W.1. (Next to the Bon Viveur.) Light green and gold outside, inside carpeted and brocaded. Opulent, but life goes on just the same. Has a genuine sedan chair for a telephoney kiosk, but survives even that.

THE DOVER CASTLE, Weymouth Mews, W.1. The saloon bar intimate, aquarium on the counter (of course somebody had to give the fishes a drink once—the gin killed the lot), stags'-antler coat hangers, log seats, shell ash trays, a display of family glass, Cries of Old London. At your elbow perhaps Carroll Gibbons, or some of the many others who make recordings at the International Broadcasting Studios nearby.

THE FITZROY TAVERN, corner of Charlotte Street and Windmill Street, W.1. Bar where money is thrown on ceiling (darts through notes) and collected at end of year for children's party. This house gives the impression of having never recovered from the hangover of November 11th, 1918. Clients have the air of the 'twenties, now somewhat querulous but the atmosphere is less inhibited than most pubs. The walls are covered with a fine collection of recruiting posters of the Kaiser's war, including the famous " Daddy, what did *you* do in the war?—" dusty Uhlans' helmets and U-boat sailors' caps which still seem damp.

THE WHEATSHEAF, Rathbone Place, W.1. Scotch house, Bogus Tudor. Respectable Bohemian. Can be interesting if you recognise faces.

THE DOG AND DUCK, Frith Street, Soho (Tottenham Court Road), W.1. Popular with the avant-garde artists of the Soho group.

THE YORK MINSTER, Dean Street, W.1. Much frequented by Frenchmen, owned by Monsieur Berlemont. First class restaurant on first floor.

SALISBURY, St. Martin's Lane, W.C.2. Situated in the heart of Theatreland, this is one of the few which retain almost intact the glitter and solidity of the Gin Palace. Frequented by the stage. You can either stand at the long curved bar or sit with a few friends in one of the intimate banquettes which line the walls.

NERONE'S, Trafalgar Square, W.C.2. Underground lounge, tables, settees and long bar for snacks. Middle-class, upholstered, spacious.

THE VILLIERS, Villiers Street, W.C.2. A pub with a past. At one time the poor man's Café Royal; now the large reception room behind is empty and ghostly. Billiards downstairs.

THE LAMB AND FLAG, Rose Street, W.C.2 (just off Garrick Street). Once named the "Bucket of Blood," a favourite of Dickens, as well as of the cock, and bare-fist fighters; this little pub, now dwarfed by the warehouses of nearby Covent Garden, has withstood the constant onslaughts of modernisation and provides an ideal setting for folk from the surrounding stagedoors. The alley entrance, a narrow weatherboarded slot, sets an almost nautical theme and, once inside, the scene is not disappointing. Oak-grained, rugged and unsophisticated, all bars are in the *Alehouse* tradition.

THE NAG'S HEAD, Covent Garden, W.C.2. See your favourite singer knock back a quick one in a somewhat dim atmosphere.

THE KEMBLE'S HEAD, Long Acre, W.C.2, at the junction with Bow Street. This pub has one great thing to commend it for it is open for more hours each day than any other. 5.0 a.m. until 9.0 a.m., 11.30 to 3.0, and in the evening 5.30 until 11.30. The extra four hours in the early morning are for the benefit of Covent Garden Market workers, but if you are studying the Market at work there should be no objection to your taking a little sustenance during your labours. The other Covent Garden pubs open half-an-hour later, at 5.30 a.m.

THE MUSEUM TAVERN, Great Russell Street, W.C.1. Solid and simple pub with good snack bar, serves meals in evening as well as lunch time. Students and intellectuals. Opposite British Museum gates.

City pubs

Lunch time and after office hours (up to 7 p.m.) trade, otherwise deserted. Very frequently they have only a six-day licence. Otherwise no different from other pubs except for the clientele and the greater accent on eating. (For a list of City chop-houses turn to 1 p.m.)

99, BISHOPSGATE, E.C.2. You want to see the City gents? Go to 99. Bowler hats in the saloon bar, messengers in the public. Popular.

DROP IN FOR A PINT at the SHIP TAVERN, Lime Street, E.C.3, then go and have a look at Leadenhall Market, like a comic opera setting; chickens, geese, fish, up to the proscenium arch.

THE CASTLE, Cowcross Street, E.C.1, near the meat market. Landlord granted a pawnbroker's licence by George IV, but present one not keen to do that kind of business these days.

OLD BELL, Fleet Street, E.C.4. Journalists' haunt. Informal and cosy, backs on to Wren's St. Bride's.

THE KING LUD, Ludgate Circus (Blackfriars), E.C.4. In the Gin Palace tradition. Abundance of decorated mirrors, screens and mahogany in a ceramic setting.

East End and riverside

As if to compensate for the bleakness and enormity of dockland (featureless roads, vast chimneys and gantries) the East End pub is usually tiny and intimate, floors sawdusted, seats and tables of scrubbed deal. There is normally only one bar, the public bar, sometimes with the addition of various rooms or compartments. The riverside pub has the addition of a balcony off the back room, hanging perilously over the mud and barges. Taking advantage of this situation the gentlemen's lavatory is normally to be found at one side of the balcony. Do not expect the balcony to be always exploited, people who live on the river probably see enough of it. The first four, north bank; the rest, south.

THE GRAPES, Narrow Street, E.14. A tiny house, public bar only, sawdust on the floor, front room and back. The back room leads on to a tiny balcony from which are suddenly seen the enormous snouts of stranded barges. From the river the house has a fine but decayed Regency effect, first floor bow window and slender glazing. Ash cans on the balcony and a typically English disregard for the attractions of the river view.

THE PROSPECT OF WHITBY, Wapping Wall, E.1. One bar, looking like advanced version of Kim's game, everything from an aquarium to assegais, pin-ups to pistols, clogs, Chianti bottles, copper kettles, skulls, old furniture and a sense of decay. Similar to Dirty Dick's in variety of items collected. Eat in the Pepys Room on the first floor. Room and balcony overlooking Limehouse Reach.

THE WHITE HART, The Highway, E.14. A bald interior but to the connoisseur of the functional tradition this is as pure as an early Delage or Bentley. Light oak graining, slender cast iron columns and a marbled bar back.

THE BLACK HORSE, Ropemaker's Fields, E.14. Typical small dockland pub. Floor covered with sawdust, narrow scrubbed benches and scrubbed tables, ceiling boarded, nicotine, walls mahogany paint, arched mahogany bar back and finest of all, a tiny Jug and Bottle department, five feet wide, separated by a partition the whole wall of which is decorated with a Mann, Crossman & Paulin sign painted in cursive shadow type which is almost illegible under coats of varnish and tobacco smoke.

THE ANCHOR, Bankside, S.E.1. The only remaining Bankside pub, Georgian and very, very nice. From here Dr. Johnson, who had rooms in the nearby Barclay's brewery, took the ferry across to the city. Apart from the concealed staircases there is a small vertical shaft giving the only access to a room in which escaped convicts from " Clink " prison, which stood nearby, took refuge . . . for a price. The Anchor is a museum example of the perfect riverside pub interior spoilt by unseemly new decorations, in this case a kind of bastard grey bleached oak grain (the old colours were an almost perfect symphony in browns). Still, when tastes change, the traditional colours can always be reinstated.

PICK UP A RIVER STEAMER and ask them to put you off at Cherry Garden Pier, or get Jim Taylor or A. Metcalf (watermen) to pick you up in a motor boat and take you to the ANGEL, Rotherhithe Stairs, S.E.16, built over the river. Ernie Reeve will make you at home. Have supper in the first floor room overlooking the river (but ring up first) and ask to see the smuggler's trapdoor in the kitchen. Room and balcony have magnificent view from Tower Bridge down to Limehouse.

TORBAY, Elephant Stairs, S.E.17. Charlie Turner to greet you. Drink your beer out on a pint-size balcony. Interested in the fight game ? Ask Bill Cottrell to show you his lads in the ring on the first floor any Monday to Friday night, 6.30 to 8.30. Danny is permanently at the piano downstairs.

THE SPREAD EAGLE AND CROWN, 117, Rotherhithe Street, S.E.16. Minute, but like the GRENADIER (which see) a top ranking example of pub vernacular. No frills, kitchen-with-a-bar type to which evolution has added a shop window. The inside wants a coat of varnish ; the outside is that rare thing, a completely untouched early pub façade. Here, if you are interested, is the missing link between the 18th-century shop or coffee-house front and the mid-Victorian pub front. No river balcony unfortunately.

further afield

THE DOVES, Upper Mall, W.6. The ideal choice for a quiet summer evening's tipple in the open air right on the river, or go at lunch time if you want to sit down. Pub itself very cosy, low ceilinged, Rowlandsonish, good example of the functional tradition. Look out for the stairs. Minute public bar.

PUB WITH A SKITTLE ALLEY. THE BLACK LION, Hammersmith, W.6. One of the many pubs with a skittle alley, but one of the more charming.

THE WHITE CROSS, St. Helena Terrace, Richmond, Surrey. Standing among the boathouses. You can sit outside or also watch the river from the raised vantage point of the small, pleasant saloon or parlour. A village pub.

THE THREE PIGEONS, Richmond, Surrey. On the towpath and up-river from the bridge. In season the large riverside terrace holds more than its fair share of children and ice-cream cartons. A good site but too popular.

THE CIDER HOUSE, Nine Elms, S.W.8. One of the few houses which sell cider almost exclusively, rough and sweet. Friendly atmosphere and a wealth of nautical bric-a-brac. Stuffed alligator. Damaged in the bombing.

THE SWAN, Stockwell, S.W.9. Noted for its singing, which you can listen to or join in with, especially Saturdays.

THE CANTON ARMS, S. Lambeth Road, S.W.8. Good singing. Rather more organized " turns." Closes 10.30, time to dash back to Westminster.

THE KING'S HEAD AND EIGHT BELLS, Cheyne Row, S.W.3. During the summer months the custom is to take your drink out of doors to backwater street and public gardens, specially Sunday mornings. Favourite scenic background of *Picture Post's* " film star with pint " features. Chelsea artists and intellectuals.

THE CROSS KEYS, Lawrence Street, S.W.3. Small, intimate, slacks and corduroys of Chelsea. Robust singing on Saturday evenings.

THE SCARSDALE ARMS, Edwardes Square, W.8. Here is ample space to sit on the rustic seats beside the pavement in a side street of this quiet square. Inside, some degree of modernisation, but the small annexe to the saloon bar still remains snug and intimate.

THE WINDSOR CASTLE, Campden Hill, W.8. Favourite of the Notting Hill Gate smart set. Settles, benches and scrubbed tables in the public bar. Walled garden, through the " Sherry " (saloon) bar very pleasant, but dependent on the weather.

THE SWAN, Bayswater Road, W.2, near Lancaster Gate. The only pub with forecourt where you can sit alongside a main thoroughfare. Here, under the striped awnings, you can watch a constant stream of traffic—both wheeled and walking. Inside there is a good snack-bar in the saloon, but for character conforming with the outside try the public bar.

THE TAVERN at Lord's Cricket Ground, N.W.8. This is the tavern adjoining the grandstand, now a famous institution. Its regulars, cricketers and fans, have formed themselves into a club. President is the Duke of Edinburgh.

ASSEMBLY HOUSE, Kentish Town Road, N.W.5. Very good example of the later Gin Palace style, the one long counter in the one large room replaced by a proliferation of bars all served from a single central area. Private bar, furtively approached down a corridor, has particularly good upholstered seating. Enormous glass windows and engraved mirrors.

WELLS, Well Walk, N.W.3. On site of old medicinal spring in charming Hampstead road. Small raised terrace for drinking in sun. Intimate and cosy.

THE VALE OF HEALTH, Hampstead Heath, N.W.3. Town pub in country-like surroundings. The pub is solid stuff and has a balcony overlooking the pond and heath. Easter and August Bank holidays the adjoining fair operates with great vigour and noise.

THE SPANIARDS, Hampstead Heath, N.W.3. Country pub style, sporting prints and old corners to sit. Excellent punctuation when visiting Kenwood House.

wine drinking

There are conventions about drinking in pubs and the person who asks for a glass of wine in a pub is likely to create one of H. M. Bateman's scenes. You may however get your favourite Sauterne or Chablis without embarrassment in a Henekey House. They specialise in wines as well as beers, and will sell wine by the glass, or a half bottle for yourself and friend.

GORDON'S, Villiers Street, W.C.2. Leaving the South Bank by the Bailey Bridge go under the railway bridge to Villiers Street and you will find a little staircase going down to Gordon's wine bar. There is no sign outside the door but don't shove off—just push. It is a tiny cellar, very full in the evenings, where you can sit and drink wines and sherries by the glass at reasonable prices. Decoration is ordinary but it has considerable atmosphere. As " Free Vintners " they need not observe ordinary opening hours—but do.

JAMAICA WINE BAR. Down an alley just off Lombard Street, E.C.3.

Ceiling of panelled lincrusta. Long vista of polished barrels; high clerestory windows. Air of warehouse. Piles of cigar boxes. You sit on champagne boxes. Accountant who looks like Bob Cratchett sits in striped trousers surrounded by bill spikes. Dark mahogany, solid functional. Baskets of wine; confusion. Parcels made up for delivery. Long bar with partitions stopping short of ceiling. Gas brackets over bar. Racks of wine.

GEOFFREY'S, Tothill Street, S.W.1. Convenient for Abbey visitors. Small room where you will be served champagnes and sherry in comfort.

7 pm

WHERE TO GO

Entertainment. This is a vast item for London. 10,000,000 people to be kept happy as well as yourself. Look at what London offers, from theatres to music halls, from concerts to jazz clubs, cinemas and broadcast shows. Can you blame us if our list is incomplete ?

Morning and evening papers will give most programmes and times. The main ticket booking agencies are Keith Prowse, 159, New Bond Street (REG. 6000) and branches (see the telephone book), Ashton and Mitchell, 2, Old Bond Street (MAY. 7222) and Theatre Tickets and Messengers, 100, St. Martin's Lane (TEM. 1023) and branches. The best reviews of new productions are those in *The Times* on the morning after opening night and in *The Observer* on Sundays.

THEATRES

Shaftesbury Avenue—Charing Cross Road, is the centre of Theatreland. Programmes are listed fully in the evening papers; reference is made here either to theatres that have some special distinguishing mark that won't be obvious to the visitor looking through a list of names ; or to those not ordinarily listed at all. Of the official theatres the doyen is :

DRURY LANE, Catherine Street, W.C.2 (TEM: 8108). First built in 17th century—destroyed by fire and rebuilt 1812. Every crowned head since Charles II has sat in the Royal Box. Dryden, Congreve and Sheridan have seen their plays presented there. Nell Gwynne, Edmund Kean and Mrs. Siddons have appeared on the bills. Still has period character (don't miss the staircase—and don't miss the ghost).

MOST SATISFYING EXTERIOR is the HAYMARKET (in the Haymarket) with its colonnade, seen at its best from St. James's Square, closing the vista down Charles II Street with the statue of William III in foreground.

THE OLD VIC, Waterloo Road, S.E.1 (WAT: 7616) of Shakespearean repertory is, of course, an institution which has achieved world renown. Was a music hall before taken on by Lilian Baylis, 1898-1937. Bombed in 1941, the Old Vic Company were in provinces; then at the NEW for 5 years and have just returned to their original theatre, redecorated, very rightly, in full-blooded red-and-gold. Have given many performances abroad, including New York, Australia, and five international festivals. Present company headed by Roger Livesey, Peggy Ashcroft, Ursula Jeans, Alec Clunes. The programme for their FESTIVAL REPERTORY SEASON (May 7 to June 30) includes Shaw's *Captain Brassbound's Conversion* (Prod: Hugh Hunt, May 7, 8, 9); *Twelfth Night* (Prod: Hugh Hunt, May 10-16, June 18-20); Jonson's *Bartholomew Fair* (Prod: Geo. Devine, May 17-23); *Henry V* (Prod: Glen Byam Shaw, May 24-29, June 21-27); *Merry Wives of Windsor* (Prod: Hugh Hunt, June 1-9, 28-30); Sophocles' *Electra* (Prod: Michel Saint Denis) and Chekov's *The Wedding* (Prod: George Devine) July 11, 12 and 13. Performances at 7.15 p.m. ; mats. Tues. and Sats. at 2.30. Seats can be booked in advance 2s. to 10s. 6d.

OPEN AIR THEATRE, Queen Mary's Gardens, Regent's Park, N.W.1 (WEL: 2060) (Baker Street Station). Founded 1933 by Robert Atkins, also of Shakespearean repertory. Opening on May 22, they will be giving *A Midsummer Night's Dream* (for at least 2 months) with Robert Atkins as Bottom, Leslie French as Puck. Seating for 2,000 and plenty of room on the grass, but get there early if it looks like rain, for the under cover theatre holds about half that number. Performances at 7.30 p.m. Mon. to Sat. with mats. 2.30 p.m. Wed., Thurs. and Sat. Prices range from 1s. 3d. to 7s. 6d.

THE SAVOY (by that hotel in the Strand, W.C.2—TEM: 8888) was traditional home of Gilbert and Sullivan light opera. A thirteen week season, starting May 7, will include *Mikado*, *Yeomen of the Guard*, *Box and Cox*, *Pirates of Penzance*, *Iolanthe*, *Patience*, *Ruddigore*, *Trial by Jury*, *H.M.S. Pinafore*, and *The Gondoliers*.

theatre clubs

Feature of theatrical life in London is existence of a number of theatre clubs, little theatres or neighbourhood theatres, which exist to make theatrical experiments. They are formed as clubs mainly because, under English law, no theatrical play may be performed in public unless it has been licensed by the Lord Chamberlain and many experimental plays fail to satisfy his highly developed sense of decorum. A performance to members of a club is not, in law, a public performance. But this is not the only reason: many of these theatres are the creation of a group of enthusiasts. Their first interest is talent. The principal theatre clubs are:

ARTS, Great Newport Street, W.C.2 (TEM: 3334) (Leicester Square Station). Has been going for 25 years. Re-formed in 1942 by Alec Clunes, opening with Clifford Odets's "Golden Boy." Puts on new plays and outstanding revivals. During May and June you can see Festival programme of Shaw's one-act plays. Performances 7 p.m. Tues. to Fri., 5 and 8 p.m. Sats. and Suns. Membership 20,000, full membership 4,500, 350 seats. Full membership would cost you £3 3s. to join and £3 3s. a year—or, if you come from overseas, £1 for 3 months —but if you don't want to use the restaurant, lounge and bar, you can become a theatre member for 5s. a year, which entitles you to buy tickets (5s., 7s. 6d. and 10s. 6d.). Write to the Secretary, Mr. M. Chaplin, or telephone him at TEM: 7541.

NEW BOLTONS, Drayton Gardens, S.W.10 (KEN: 5898) (S. Kensington Station and 30 bus down Old Brompton Road). Peter Cotes took over this little (240 seat) theatre last November and plans to put on plays of consequence, whether old or new. As contribution to the Festival, has put on in May and June, Shelley's "The Cenci" with Joan Miller as Beatrice. Performances 8 p.m. Tues. to Suns. and at 5 p.m. on Sats and Suns. Full member £1 1s., theatre member 5s. Tickets 2s. 6d., 5s., 7s. 6d. Telephone the theatre, or get a membership form from the box office.

NEW LINDSAY, 81, Palace Gardens Terrace, W.8 (BAY: 6024) (Queensway or High Street Kensington Stations). Directors: J. A. Munro (Managing) and M. E. Corpel (Agent for French artists). Leased to Paris Plays (until October) who are putting on English adaptations of French plays; 3 weeks run each play. Have recently put on "Frou-Frou" with Jean Kent, and Roger Ferdinand's "Husbands Don't Count," adapted by Patricia Hollender, with Edwin Styles, Winifred Shotter, Jean Cadell and Gabriel Brune. Many shows go on to the West End and/or on tour. Performances 8 p.m. Tues. to Fri.; 5 and 8 p.m. Sats. and Suns. Membership 5s. a year and seats from 3s. 6d. to 10s. 6d. (bookable 24 hours in advance). Telephone, or apply at box office to join.

PLAYERS, Villiers Street, W.C.2 (TRA: 1134) (Charing Cross Station). Started in 1936, is now produced by Don Gemmel, who also acts as Chairman to this revival of Victorian Music Hall—"The Late Joys." Programme changes once a fortnight, with the occasional addition of a short Victorian melodrama or opera, and after the show there is dancing on the stage until midnight. Here you can sit at a table, drink your beer and eat your sandwiches while watching the show—for a full meal you'll have to go to the supper room. Performances 8 p.m. on Mon. and Tues., 9 p.m. Weds. to Sat. The snag is that to join you have to be proposed by a member of over a year's standing. Entrance fee £2 2s. and annual subscription £3 3s. But if you're an overseas visitor, telephone the secretary, Miss Barren, and ask if you can join—30s. for 3 months or 7s. 6d. a week. Members don't pay for seats, but pay 5s. for each friend taken with them.

UNITY, Goldington Street, N.W.1 (EUS: 5391) (Mornington Crescent Station). With a political bias to the left and strictly amateur performances (only their administrative staff is paid) which normally run for 6½ weeks. Their Festival show is "The Work of the King" (based on the peasant revolt of 1381), adapted by Charles Poulsen from his book *English Episode*, and produced by Richard Hayter. Most of their members come from affiliated organisations—Trade Unions, and they also have an Amateur Mobile Theatre which gives performances at various Trade Unions, etc., on request. Performances 7.30 p.m., Wednesdays to Sundays. Membership is 2s. 6d. a year and seats bookable (2s. to 5s.). Telephone, or apply at the box office to join, but give 48 hours' notice before you want to buy a ticket.

WATERGATE, 29, Buckingham Street, W.C.2 (TRA: 6261) (Charing Cross Station). Opened in November, 1949. Directors: Elizabeth Denby, Velona Pilcher (Founder-Director of the old Gate Theatre which was bombed during the war) and Elizabeth Sprigge. Plays by new writers; readings of un-

published plays; films, lectures and discussions; chamber concerts; and late night revues "for those with a distaste for the priggish." Name of the theatre comes from the Inigo Jones Water Gate (see 8 a.m.) at the end of the road. Murals in theatre by Marc Chagall and club rooms show works of other contemporary artists. Times of performances vary; usually 7 to 7.30 p.m. with the revues at 10.30 p.m., and about half an hour earlier on Sundays. Prices of tickets also vary, from 3s. to 10s. 6d. Full membership costs £1 1s. a year and special arrangements are made for students and overseas visitors. Apply to the Secretary, Mrs. Siddons.

out of town theatres

Not so well known are the theatres just outside the central area. Some are experimental theatres, with managements anxious to discover new talent among dramatists, and many of the plays produced subsequently have runs in the West End. Since these theatres are within London they are generally able to assemble a cast of first rate quality. All are worth investigating. They are:

Q THEATRE, Kew Bridge, Brentford (CHI: 2920). Once a drill hall, opened in 1929 by Jack de Leon and sister. Since staged over 1,000 new plays and revivals. Performances 8 p.m.

LYRIC, Hammersmith, W.6 (RIV: 4432). Once a flamboyant "blood club." Nigel Playfair spotted it in 1918 and kicked off with 1,463 performances of the *Beggars Opera*. Performances 7 p.m.

OTHERS ARE: EMBASSY, Swiss Cottage, N.W.8 (PRI: 2311). Performances 7.45 p.m. (not Mondays). KING'S, Hammersmith, S.W.6 (RIV: 5094). Performances 7 p.m. NEW THEATRE, Bromley (Station: Bromley North, S.R.) (RAV: 6677). Performances 7.45 p.m. RICHMOND THEATRE, The Green, Richmond (RIC: 0088). Performances 7.45 p.m. (Saturdays 8.15 p.m.).

circuit theatres

Then there are the circuit theatres, that is, theatres at which a touring company plays in a London success for a week or a fortnight at a time.

THESE ARE: CROYDON GRAND, High Street, Croydon (CRO: 0011) (Station: East Croydon, S.R.). GOLDERS GREEN HIPPODROME, Golders Green, N.W.11 (SPE: 0022) (Station: Golders Green underground). STREATHAM HILL THEATRE, Streatham Hill, S.W.2 (TUL: 3331) (Station: Streatham S.R.). WIMBLEDON THEATRE, S.W.19 (LIB: 1166) (Station: Wimbledon).

opera and ballet

The extra special opera and ballet in London is at COVENT GARDEN OPERA HOUSE but the home of ballet is the SADLER'S WELLS THEATRE. Its management is linked with that of the Old Vic. The most romantic of our opera houses is to be found at GLYNDEBOURNE in Sussex. Thence, of a Summer evening, streams of stuffed shirts and bare shoulders pour in trains and cars out of the West End.

ROYAL OPERA HOUSE, Covent Garden (TEM: 7961). First opened 1732. Handel conducted the " Messiah " there, and Weber the opera " Oberon " in 1826. Burnt down, rebuilt for £300,000 and burnt down again. Present house designed by E. M. Barry, to rival La Scala, Milan, and called Royal Italian Opera House. Its present title acquired in 1892. Diaghilev's Russian ballet company performed there in 1911. Bought by the Government and now controlled by the Arts Council.

SADLER'S WELLS, Rosebery Avenue, E.C.1 (TER: 1672). Cheapest seat 1s. 6d., based on the price of ten cigarettes (a condition of Trust Deed is that cheapest seats should be within means of artisans, and this is the test). Mineral spring discovered on the site 1683, exploited by Sadler with additional attraction of " musick house." Theatre built 1765, rebuilt 1931, but if you're very keen, the manager will show you the old well—through trap doors at back of the pit. One time home of Sadler's Wells Ballet (now at Covent Garden) and still the home of the Junior team. The mixed Opera/Ballet programme for the Festival season includes Purcell's *Dido and Aeneas* and the ballet *Pineapple Poll*, with sets and costumes designed by Osbert Lancaster.

GLYNDEBOURNE, Elizabethan manor house on Sussex downs 60 miles from London, where John L. Christie built a 600-seat opera house (stage bigger than auditorium). Rudolph Bing (now at the Metropolitan, New York) was one time administrator. Noted since 1934 for opera, especially Mozart. Season this year (June 20 to July 21) opens with " Idomeneo," followed by " Marriage of Figaro," " Cosi fan Tutti " and " Don Giovanni "; produced by Carl Ebert and orchestra conducted by Fritz Busch. Catch the opera train, 3.45 or 4.45 from Victoria, " evening dress very strongly requested." Opera starts 5.30, finishing about 10, with interval of from one to two hours. Wander round the beautiful gardens during interval and/or have dinner. If you have time, spare five minutes for the 18th century church in Glynde. Back in London by 11.30. Warning, minimum price £1 1s. (most seats at 2 and 3 guineas). Book seats at usual agencies, or from Dean & Dawson, 23, Baker Street, W.1 (WEL: 0092), who sell the combined train and bus tickets (13s. 2d. for 3rd class return.)

music halls

Believe it or not London's music halls started out as pubs. Tavern theatres (some of which went back to before 1580) were encouraged to multiply under the disguise of the pub, owing to Acts of Parliament, which put an embargo on unlicensed dramatic performances in the nineteenth century. Famous halls like the Britannia, the Canterbury, and Evans Song and Supper Rooms became so large they either swallowed the parent pub, or sported one as a mere appendage, but the cabaret tradition continued. It was not until the twentieth century that eating and drinking in the auditorium was made illegal, thereby utterly destroying the spirit if not entirely the outward form, of this great tradition. With the coming of microphone and the revolutionary change in popular music even the form has now all but gone. However, there will still be a few turns that recall a style of humour and

voice production made all the more fascinating to the curious for being sandwiched between crooners, tap dancers and imitation Bob Hopes. And there are still, of course, the acrobats. For the full flavour (fixed on canvas for ever by Walter Sickert) you will have to leave the West End for the jungle of Poplar or Islington. Three most characteristic of the old tradition are Collins's, near the Angel, Islington; The Queen's, Poplar, and the Metropolitan, Edgware Road. In these what remains of a close contact between bar and stage is all that is left to us of the great days—except an atmosphere.

COLLINS'S. Founded as an extension of the Landsdowne Tavern by Sam Collins, the Irish comedian, in 1861. Little altered since 1897. Electricity there is, but still combined (anyway in the bare brick passages) with flaring gas jets in open wire cages. Auditorium is in plush and a modified though gilded rococo. Watch part of performance anyway through glass screen at back of stalls, while drinking in the bar (though a net curtain is in the way, presumably as concession to the law). Pay particular attention to the old advertisements, playbills, photographs and paintings which give you a potted history of the hall; most recent local boy to make good is Tommy Trinder. Typical programme (typical for other minor halls, too, since most of these productions go the rounds): The New 1951 Edition of *Fig Leaves and Apple Sauce* (*In Autumn the leaves begin to fall!*). A Grand Fast-Moving Production in 1 scenes! Featuring Harry Prince, the Popular Radio and Revue Comedian; The "Fig Leaf" Girls; Sheba, The Queen of Dancing Tease—Exotic and Delightful; Camille, Art and Glamour, and so on. Proprietor is Lew Lake; at Islington Green, N.1. (CAN. 3251). Monday to Friday shows are continuous from 6.15; Saturday, 6.15 to 8.25. Prices up to 3s.

THE METROPOLITAN. Opened in 1862, was an outgrowth of the White Lion pub. Little changed inside or out, and you can still watch the performance from the bar; the bill is more sophisticated than the others, owing to a too-close proximity to the West End. In the Edgware Road, W.2. (AMB. 2478). Manager, Albert E. Vasco. Performances Monday to Friday 6.30 and 8.45. Saturday ten minutes earlier. Prices from 9d. to 5s.

THE QUEEN'S. Built in the '60s and originally known as the Apollo. Still has a nice glass wall to its bar through which you can watch show obliquely in a Sickert-like posture. Too restrained in decoration; less restrained in audience and reaction; public drawn from the real East End and well worth visiting for themselves. Director Maurice Abrahams has been manager there for 40 years—a family management started by his father, Michael Abrahams, about 50 years ago. Gracie Fields gave first London performance at Queen's, Poplar High Street, E.14 (EAS. 3393). Monday to Friday, continuous from 6.20; Saturday, 6.15 and 8.20. Prices from 1s. to 3s., or a box.

variety theatres

Top West-End variety theatre is the Palladium. Features the best talent available from old and new world; not forgetting Hollywood's stream of stars. Personal appearance of celluloid dummies in full horror of dimensions is pleasingly shocking to English taste. Spiritual home of Danny Kaye who celebrates here periodically more than Roman triumphs. Argyle Street, W.1. (GER. 7373); station: Oxford Circus. The other standing variety dish (though of a later vintage) is The Windmill—We Never Closed—as if you hadn't heard. It is a small house with variety turns interspersed (to the greater interest of the majority of its patrons) with well-displayed feminine beauty. On a board outside you will find the names of comedians (and others) whose name the Windmill has made. At Great Windmill Street, W.1 (GER. 7413). Non-stop variety from midday to last complete show at 9.0.

CINEMAS

Cinemas are simple if you know how film distribution works. Like this:—Films first appear at premier (or first-run) houses, big cinemas in the West End; prices are high. When they have had a season there (depending on their popularity), they usually go to the second-run houses, the Odeon and the Dominion in Tottenham Court Road, the New Victoria and Metropole in Victoria, a little less expensive. Here films run for a week, after which they go to the circuit cinemas, first for a week in the north-west suburbs, for the second week to the north-east and the third and final week's screening in the south. If you consistently forget to go and see the film you have been meaning to see during these four weeks your last chance (if it's one of the better films) is to see it at one of the revival cinemas (some even in the West End, such as Rialto, Astoria and Tatler). Not falling into any of these categories are the cinemas showing foreign films. Prices vary (mostly high) and the film is unlikely to be shown again (so if you don't see it you've had it). Some of these cinemas also combine a good revival (perhaps a Charlie Chaplin or other pre-war classic) in the programme. Here's a short list of the foreign-film houses: Academy and Studio One in Oxford Street, usually the best bet; Cameo-Polytechnic in Regent Street; Continentale in Tottenham Court Road; Classic in Chelsea; Everyman, Hampstead; the Curzon in Curzon Street is the arm-chaired snob cinema for foreign films. The first public film show was given where now stands the Cameo-Polytechnic in Regent Street. The oldest cinema (as such) in London is The Biograph (a generic name in fact, coming historically between Bioscope and Cinema), in Vauxhall Bridge Road. Fame has by-passed it and it now shows Westerns to a local Pimlico clientele. Nothing remains of the gas lighting, orchestra pit, and red plush, but the projection room is still called the Bio Box and (architecturally) the two cast iron pillars supporting the box remain. The most startling interior is possibly the Gaumont, Notting Hill Gate; the biggest, the Gaumont State in Kilburn.

broadcasting

Walking down Lower Regent Street you come upon the Paris Cinema. No film advertised. Why? Because it isn't a cinema but an offshoot of the BBC—the place from which they broadcast variety programmes. Private of course, but you can get in, though it will take about three weeks to arrange, so arrange it if possible before you come to London. Other BBC programmes open to ticket-holders (some light and a little serious music) are from studios at Aeolian Hall, Bond Street; and 201, Piccadilly—there's not much at BBC itself. Write saying what programme you want to see to Ticket Unit, BBC, Portland Place, W.1; only one double ticket to each applicant. (Public not allowed at present to television.)

recording

Another private show you may get into as a special favour, is the Star Recording Studios. Mr. Faraday, the manager, will probably let you have a peep at the working of the busiest private recording studio in this country. Special effects, gramophone, film and broadcasting work catered for. Typical day's work might include editing a radio programme for Australia in the morning, recording little dogs barking for a theatre sound effect in the afternoon; later the recording of a Handel oratorio for America, and an evening audience show for Radio Luxemburg. The hall seats 450. Layout:— Recording room on the left of the stage, extra studio off left hand door on stage. At the back of the hall, the control room fronted by the executives' box (where the few lucky people can hear the show as it will come out over your loudspeaker). At Rodmarton Mews, Blandford Street, W.1. If not just one of the idly curious, ring Mr. Faraday (LAN. 2201).

jazz clubs

There are two distinct categories of music under the term jazz, New Orleans and Bebop. Bebop is a modern derivative but you will have to get the technical explanation from some one else. Even then it's possible that you (as we) will remain a square (someone who doesn't understand). Suffice it to say that they are different and hate each other. Dress for attending jazz clubs: men wear crepe-soled shoes, gaberdines if possible, check shirts, loud ties; ladies look smart, wear modified cocktail dresses, low-heeled shoes (ballet shoes, without the block best, if you intend to dance). Those present are split up into dancers and listeners. For the square we recommend listening, but a serious concentrated look and a steady beat with the right foot will make you look like an old timer. Both the band and dancers are well worth watching. You will get soft drinks (cola varieties) with straws and sandwiches at any club. Procedure for getting into jazz clubs: strictly speaking a member's introduction is needed but don't let that hold you back as someone will always oblige. Price round about 5s. Undoubtedly the best attraction is Humphrey Lyttelton (old Etonian) at the London Jazz Club, 100, Oxford Street, W.1. Saturdays and Mondays, 7.30-11.0. Busiest spot, the London Studios, 10-11, Gt. Newport Street, with one club or another practically every night, including South American varieties. For the low-down on the week's jazz programmes at the various London clubs, buy the *Melody Maker*, any Friday.

CONCERTS

A feast of music is being turned on for Bach devotees, Tschaikovskyites, modernists, discord-lovers and others. Hundreds of programmes have been planned for your careful sifting. These range from large orchestral concerts to one-man recitals, from choirs of a thousand voices to 16th century madrigal singing. Special attention is being paid to our own neglected composers, led by our greatest ever—versatile, scholarly, dignified Ralph Vaughan Williams. See concerts section in *The Times* or *The Daily Telegraph* on Saturdays, or *London Musical Events* (monthly, 1s.).

ROYAL FESTIVAL HALL. South Bank, Festival Site, S.E.1 (WAT. 3191) (Waterloo Station). The new hall was opened in the presence of Royalty at a ceremonial concert on May 3rd. Seven inaugural concerts (May 4th-9th) and from May 10th-June 30th concerts will be held here every evening—orchestral, choral, chamber music and recitals. From July 1st-October 24th three series of eight orchestral concerts each will be given on Wednesday and Sunday evenings by the London Philharmonic, London Symphony and Philharmonia Orchestras. We advise you to book early, particularly if your purse is slender, as there has been a great demand for tickets for the more popular concerts and in quite a few cases only the more expensive seats remain (7s. 6d. and upwards). The hall seats approximately 3,000 and all evening concerts start at 8.0 (except May 4th, 8.30). Seats (ordinary concerts) from 2s. 6d.-12s. 6d.

ROYAL ALBERT HALL, Kensington Gore, S.W.7 (KEN. 8212) (South Kensington Station). Colossus of London halls, with impressive amphitheatre. A big programme of orchestral and choral concerts has been arranged. The Royal Philharmonic Orchestra, conducted by Beecham and Stokowski, will give eight orchestral concerts from May 11th-June 17th and the Royal Choral Society four choral concerts on May 10th, 17th, 24th and June 9th. A Festival of English Song and Dance will be held from June 21st-23rd. This is the home of the popular B.B.C. Summer Promenade Concerts Season which will take place from July 28th-September 22nd. Boasts one of the largest and finest organs in the world. If the walls of Jericho toppled at the sound of the trumpets and the shouting, then these should certainly crumble to dust when the stops are pulled right out. Hall holds about 8,000, so you should normally find no difficulty in getting in. Price of seats ranges from 2s. upwards.

WIGMORE HALL, Wigmore Street, W.1 (WEL. 2141) (Oxford Circus Station). Main hall for chamber music and recitals, which are held regularly. A series of concerts of English Song has been arranged for May 7th, 14th, 21st, 28th, June 4th, 11th. There is also a series tracing the development of English Music from 1300 to 1750 on May 9th, 16th, 23rd, 30th, June 6th, 13th, 27th. Smallish and cosy, seats 540.

CENTRAL HALL, Westminster, S.W.1 (WHI. 4259) (St. James's Park Station). Various orchestral, choral and chamber music concerts and recitals have been arranged. Sir Robert Mayer's Children's Concerts take place on Saturday mornings on May 19th, June 2nd, 16th and 30th. Seats 2,700.

KINGSWAY HALL, Kingsway, W.C.2 (HOL. 3246) (Holborn Station). Orchestral concerts, chamber music and recitals will be given. Seats 1,800.

8 pm

DINNER OUT

Let's face it, good food costs money in any part of the western world today. Rude things are said about English cooking, particularly by the English, but we hold that if you are prepared to pay French prices you can get as good (French) food in London as in Paris. The places in France today where you can eat well cheaply are about as many as the pennies you pay for the meat ration. Mere window-dressing is the official table d'hôte menu of say 450 frs. in which the inedible " veal " is no more agreeable than cottage pie. The French gain is in cheap but drinkable wine, without which no meal can be a banquet, and a tradition of style which moves even the meanest restaurant proprietor to provide an endless series of clean plates at an expense of spirit in respect to washing up, that the English, who grudge you even a knife for your sandwich in a pub, simply do not begin to compete with. The wine in some English restaurants in 1951 is both new and expensive, but for summer, wine- or cider-cups provide a delicious alternative, and of course the iced lagers and bottled beers of Bass/Worthington quality are supreme. Wine is drawn attention to in the notes which follow only because the visitor from abroad is likely to find the price of it his worst headache. A vin rosé en carafe might cost 2s. in the South of France (a price all good Frenchmen regard as monstrous) — anything from 15s. upwards in London, which doesn't make sense. All the same, you can eat in a very civilized way, and in all the restaurants mentioned here food will be good anyway and in many cases superlative. Which goes also for those listed under the restaurants in the night-club section and under 1 p.m.—most of which, don't forget, are open for dinner too. For instance, the oyster bars, very pleasant on a warm evening. By the way, don't forget the restaurants at the Festival. Last word in decoration, the Regatta, with a tremendous view of St. Paul's.

PÈRE AUGUSTE (LE CHÂTELAIN) 37, Gerrard Street, W.1 GER : 3878	Monsieur Auguste, white goatee'd and alert, will recommend (if you are a man) the pâté maison and the cold veal and ham pie, both specialities. Excellent cold table as well as French menu; décor, Cole's red striped wall paper, style Edward VII. Try the Château Petit-village 1943 if your purse is lined; if not there is drinkable carafe wine at 10s. which is cheaper than you get almost anywhere else. Père Auguste believes in wine and makes it possible for you to get it, so three cheers for Père Auguste.
AKROPOLIS 24, Percy Street, W.1 MUS : 2289	One of the true homes of the Moussaka when in season (it needs marrows and aubergines). Bright and noisy.
L'APERITIF GRILL 102, Jermyn Street, W.1 WHI : 1571	Convenient. French cuisine. No music or dancing.
BELLE MEUNIÈRE 5, Charlotte Street, W.1 MUS : 4975	Décor near modern, white walls, pink lights, pink carpets. Bar at the back. Doorman. Waiters white-jacketed. Very good food cooked personally for you (specialities, escalope maison, viane de boeuf biane, crêpe suzette). ALC, average about 15s. Carafe of red wine at 14s. 6d. Personal service from proprietors Mario and Gaspar.
BOULESTIN 23, Southampton Street, Strand, W.C.2 TEM : 7061	Ornate, elaborate red, and very good. Monsieur Boulestin is a famous gastronome who writes widely telling the British how not to eat. You are likely to do yourself more than well here for they understand food. Don't hurry over dinner.
CAFÉ ROYAL 68, Regent Street, W.1 REG : 8240	One of the tragedies, decoratively speaking of gastronomic London. In the naughty nineties and up to after World War I the Café Royal *WAS* Bohemia. Its tables are festooned with shades—of everybody who ever was anybody in the artistic and literary world, from Oscar Wilde to Augustus John. Then for reasons which still remain mysterious, golden ornaments, caryatids, wall mirrors, the whole ornate interior, was replaced by jazz-modern decorations (and now redone in Empire style). The grill-room was spared. So if you want to see what we mean visit both. The genteel grill-room colours are new, but isn't this otherwise just what a grill-room should look like, what the Café Royal should look like ? Our prayer is that one day they will restore the café to its original decorative scheme.

LA COQUILLE 79, St. Martin's Lane, W.C.2. TEM : 8768	Capable of producing both good food and good wine. Gay, cosy bar in the ground floor restaurant round which Frenchmen congregate. Decorations in better taste than some we could mention.
CRETE 19, Percy Street, W.1. MUS : 4914	Greek. Has become the second of the two best Greek restaurants. The red vin ordinaire is very drinkable and amongst the cheapest at 12s. 6d.
ENCLOSURE RESTAURANT Empire Stadium, Wembley, Middx. WEM : 1234	Mondays, Thursdays, Saturdays only. Attraction here is greyhound and speedway racing. 8s. enclosure fee. Ring up WEM : 1234 to book a table high in the glass-walled grandstand. They are all for four, in three tiers, the lowest tier the most exciting. Menu, TDH is 7s. 6d. First race 7.30, but get there earlier to bet, and watch the eight races from your table. Your bets will be placed for you (2s. and up); biggest (tote) clock in Britain will give you the results. Fine view over reporters, judges, bookies, and of course the track. Direct communication to trackside for close-up view. Floor below, longest bar in Europe. Bakerloo to Wembley Central (Watford Line) with a ten minutes walk, or to Wembley Park (Stanmore Line) with alternative 5 minute walk or 2d. bus ride along the Empire Way.
ESCARGOT 48, Greek Street, W.1 GER : 4460	Very French both in its food and its atmosphere, though, again, the latter's difficult to define. No difficulty about the food, and the wine is kept, very sensibly, in ground floor cellar open to restaurant, thus ensuring room temperature. They love you to see it, so give the wine-waiter a hint if he doesn't give you one. Filled to ceiling with bins, 12 bottles each of everything. The dearest old French waiters, and caricatures and sketches of the 1900's.
L'ÉTOILE 30, Charlotte Street, W.1 MUS : 7189	Exterior the most truly Montparnassian of all the Soho restaurants, with an interior impossible to analyse or even label (but mostly cream). The connoisseur can only salute the good things that go with it. Don't let its deceptive air of ingenuousness lead you to think L'Étoile the place for a one and ninepenny ordinary.
FRASCATI 32, Oxford Street, W.1. MUS : 7414	Popular, garish, not expensive and rather enjoyable. Dancing.
JARDIN DES GOURMETS 5, Greek Street, W.1 GER : 1816	Comfort and plan (of wall settees) as much above the average as the food. Here you can eat very well indeed and the wine is reasonably priced for London. No unattached tables out in the middle, everyone's back securely attached to a wall—keynote of cosy luxury well maintained.
MAISON BASQUE 11, Dover Street, W.1 REG : 2651	Highly select and intimate, food of the very best. Dine here if you want a long and leisurely dinner without interruptions, money no object. Background is French conception of rustic, so popular now, alas, all over France.
MARTINEZ 25, Swallow Street, W.1 REG : 5066	In the Andalusian Sherry Lounge the sherry wagon will be wheeled round to your chair. Restaurant on first floor. On the way up you run the gauntlet of Spanish paintings. Upstairs it's all tiles, fountains and a bull's head, presented by Don Pedro Domenco in 1927. Another place where they make a big effort with the wine. Half a carafe at 4s. 9d., a glass at 2s., is by English standards stupendously cheap. Menu is in Spanish and English. Try tortilla, it's very typical.

MAJORCA 66, Brewer Street, W.1 GER : 6803	Famous pre-war as one of the few places you could get white Valdepeñas, that excellent wine. When you visit try the vin ordinaire, from the Madrid hills. M. Bonafont is Spanish, so are waiters, food. A Majorcan windmill (made in England), pantile roof, flower-potted iron-barred window, and " in-the-patio " decorations sound awful but aren't. This is in fact one of the nicest interiors in London. Dinner TDH at 7s. 6d. (and a very good 5s. lunch on the same terms), or your choice (Portuguese tastes also catered for, wine and food).
OVERTON'S 4, Victoria Buildings, S.W.1 VIC : 3774	Another spot very much in the Edwardian tradition—within sprinting distance of Victoria Station and the Victoria Palace of Crazy Gang fame. Mine host at Overton's is the débonair Lt.-Colonel Geoffrey Russell Hay, at one time acknowledged to be one of the best-dressed officers in the British Army. Good cuisine and good wines at not immoderate charges. Specialize in sea food downstairs in the oyster bar. We suppose we ought to have included it amongst the luncheon (sea-food) places but is best at night when you can look out on the lights of London. It has genuine character.
QUO VADIS 26, Dean Street, W.1 GER : 4809	Mr. Leoni, who has personally looked after his clients since 1926, named his restaurant after reading the book. Mainly Italian cooking, TDH dinner 9s. 6d.; but, highly recommended, tagliatelle, ravioli (made on the premises), lasagne (origin, Bologna), suprême de volaille Yolando (breast of chicken is just the beginning of this dish). The carafe wine, at 16s. 6d. *is* Chianti.
REGGIORI'S 1-3, Euston Road, N.W.1 TER : 6264	If the grill-room at the Café Royal means anything to you (in other words if you are a romantic) try Reggiori's, opposite St. Pancras, for breaths of Edwardian nostalgia. Here, but for absence of gaslight, is the atmosphere—mosaic floor, flowered and ornamental tile-and-mirror walls, brass hat pegs like spiders, brass door knobs, light fittings, hand rails and glitter to bar counter. Light fittings are like the old Pullman cars, gas jets still visible. Red plush settees (very comfortable), tables resplendent with cruets (silvered, with spaces for six articles of condiment). Reverend and old world, the waiters are Poles, Czechs, Italians and Swiss Italians (last two dominant). Mr. Capponi or one of his sons will be at the till at the far (we do mean far) end, and if you are really interested he may let you go and look at the fountain. Edgar Wallace was a regular here.
SCOTT'S Coventry Street, W.1 GER : 7175	Though you can get any kind of food here it's really one of the fishy places—in fact *the* original fishy place. If you want the biggest oysters, reddest lobsters, Scott's the place. Ought really to have been included with luncheon under sea-foods, but it happens to be at its best in the gloaming. If not at the bar, choose a window table and enjoy a free pyrotechnic display as the lights chase each other round Piccadilly Circus.
SEVENTEEN Curzon Street, W.1 MAY : 1601	A fire if it's chilly with sofas by it, with tables and settees along walls, wagon bar and outsize bottles on Georgian mantelpieces mounted with gilt mirrors, create the private house atmosphere which ought to be called the Curzon Street style. Characteristic colour : Queen Anne green with green, pink sconces. Try the Kebab and the Terrine. High marks for a good vin rosé en carafe at 15s.
SOCIETY 40, Jermyn Street, S.W.1. REG : 0565	Very elect, with real period candlelight and real period panelling. Cheque book. Music only.

9 pm

unprintable and
PRINTED

Whether you're after watching a paper go to press, or just want to hear someone air his views on the present political situation, you couldn't do better than choose 9.0 p.m. for these investigations in the metropolis. Most national papers have facilities for showing you round their works, though when they get harassed they sometimes pretend that they're full up.

TO PRESS

The fact is, most papers are rather busy, and so they won't be mad to show you round, but then if you are keen (and a genuine Festival visitor) almost all of them will weaken if you ask nicely. You may know roughly how it all works (but don't think it's like anything you have ever seen on American films). If they say to be there at 9.30 (for instance) do be punctual for your own good, because if you're five minutes late the edition will have gone to press and you may just walk through a series of rooms, empty, except for mechanics drinking tea. You will probably be seeing the first edition go to press and you will follow the printing process from the linotype machines, on the top floor. It will be a pie (jumble) line that the compositor sets for your benefit. The presses will probably inspire you most. Look out for the machine minders. These connoisseurs, one to a machine, are the highest paid workers—£4-£5 per night. Watch how they scrutinise a copy of the paper, for defects unnoticeable to you. Before you leave, you may be given a copy of your paper—that will be about 11.30 p.m. Should you happen to pass an *Evening News* delivery van you can impress your friends by giving the mudguard a bash with your fists (without injury to yourself). The secret: the mudguards are made of rubber. (But a very few of the *Evening News* vans still have metal mudguards so do be careful: anyway, that element of risk should make it exciting.)

EVENING STANDARD. Write to J. R. Robertson (Personal Assistant to General Manager). Times: 10 a.m. or 2 p.m. Give at least 1 week's notice. Tour takes 1½ hours. Parties up to 15 persons. 47, Shoe Lane, E.C.4.

NEWS OF THE WORLD. Write to the Manager. Times: 6.45 every Saturday. Not more than 12 people. Tour takes 1 hour. 30, Bouverie Street, E.C.4.

DAILY MAIL. Write to the Mechanical Department, New Carmelite House. Times: 9.30 p.m. any day except Saturdays. Parties up to 12. Give at least two months' notice. Northcliffe House, Tudor Street, E.C.4.

NEWS CHRONICLE (9.15 p.m.) and THE STAR (2.15 p.m.). Write to T. W. Parsons. Book well in advance. Tour takes 1½ hours (every day except Wed. and Sat.). Parties up to 20 persons (must be over 12 years of age). 12-22, Bouverie Street, E.C.4.

THE UNOFFICIAL WORD

" And this, my friends, is the proof of my argument." The scene Hyde Park, near Marble Arch, and the speaker on birth control has just pointed to a Salvation Army meeting near him. It is dark and, along the wide sweep of pavement with the trees of the park behind, there are clusters of people; at the centre of each cluster someone is talking and talk provokes argument. Often it is difficult to tell who is the speaker and who the citizen who disagrees, but usually it is all conducted with seriousness and good humour. Over there is a small group round an Irishman who recalls the exploits of the I.R.A. in 1939 in a song, the chorus of which ends with " And my ould alarum clock." Further on an intense young man expounds his ideas on love: surprisingly few sniggers. Whilst many of the speakers simply stand on the ground, others bring a sort of folding pulpit which carries a suitable slogan. The speakers are well known and have their own characteristics which are eagerly awaited by the regulars.

Benevolent policemen act as a safeguard against sedition and blasphemy. Some of the more serious movements avoid Hyde Park since it is so well known that it is a joke, but in central London it is the main centre for private and public discussion.

TOWER HILL (mainly at lunch times). Here you will be told the reason for emptiness of soul or pocket.

TREBOVIR ROAD, EARLS COURT (evenings). Political. *Prince Teck* across the road for those who want to conclude the inconclusive.

TRAFALGAR SQUARE, (Sunday afternoons, occasionally). Large scale political or social demonstrations. This is the traditional platform (on the plinth of Nelson's column) for the airing of policies to mass audiences. The proceedings are usually the culmination of a demonstration march through London. It has witnessed the struggles of such varied personalities as Mrs. Pankhurst, Keir Hardie and Dick Sheppard. Usually not as cold as Red Square, nor as hot as the Piazza del Popolo, but you can get wet through from the fountains. In the ordinary way the square provides a meeting place for the human and ornithological citizens of London. This recognition is aided and perpetuated by peanut vendors and photographers.

CHARING CROSS ROAD (behind the National Portrait Gallery). A rather different spectacle, that of Physical Energy and Dexterity, can be witnessed under the statue of Irving. It really amounts to oratory, since it is so much easier to describe how hard it is to tear a telephone directory in half than to do it. Neurotics who have a morbid interest in being tied-up will enjoy the chained Tarzan who wriggles out of a sack.

FURTHER OUT of London. Hampstead Heath (Whitestone Pond, Sunday morning), attracts the old and young to sample the fresh air of the Heath, and political speakers are fond of an audience. Perhaps, owing to the district, the meetings are slightly more intellectual and acrid than elsewhere. Worth going to for the scenery alone.

IN GENERAL most boroughs recognize the need for public discussion and permit it in a suitable place. If you want to hold a public meeting in the street or open place, you have to apply to the police for permission; when they refuse it is usually on the grounds of causing obstruction or nuisance. But the recognized places seem to have become open through usage. The police don't insist that you hold a meeting at such and such a place; you can apply for permission anywhere.

IN THE SUMMER MONTHS Russell Square sports a Punch and Judy show for the children (one of the few squares that attempts to provide entertainment as well as relaxation for the citizen).

PUBLIC ORATORY of the most reprehensible type is sometimes to be heard from blaring loud speaker vans, which travel at a maddeningly slow pace through quiet neighbourhoods, a practice which in our view should be punishable by deportation.

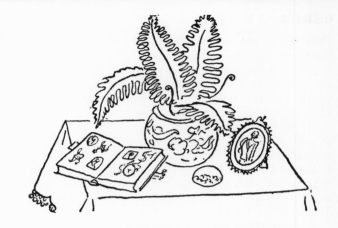

10 pm

TIME TO TURN IN

We in these islands are perhaps neither early risers (see 6.0 a.m.) nor early goers to bed. But most of our night life takes place behind doors. Thus, as taxis begin to gang up for their last battle with the theatre and cinema fans, and the pubs fill for their ultimate hour, the pavements tend to get more empty. Symbolical of this is :

CEREMONY OF THE KEYS

Only night-time ceremony remaining to London (Crying the Watch at Ely Place and others all discontinued during the war, not restarted) is now the ceremonial locking up of the Tower of London for the night. Spectators watch from the inside and are then let out through the wicket gate, re-entry only possible with the password, only known to residents, H.M. the King and the Lord Mayor. Be there at 9.40, in time for a fatherly explanation of the ensuing events by a yeoman warder (they used to buy the job for £390 but now time-expired warrant officers and N.C.O's), resplendent in long red coat and pre-Elizabethan hat. By seven minutes to ten you will have been shepherded to the Bloody Tower where four bearskinned guards will be standing at ease, waiting to escort the keys. Soldier without rifle carries ornate candle-powered lantern given him by a warder, who then marches with them down to the entrance, locks that and then gates of the Middle Tower and Byward Tower, each taking about as long as it takes to close the doors and swing down the bar. (The four soldiers, at each gate in turn presenting arms, a formalized version of the olden days " at the ready " in case of trouble.) At the Bloody Tower the detail is challenged by sentry: " Halt ", " Detail halt "," Who goes there? ", " Keys ", " Whose keys? ", " King George's keys ", " Pass King George's keys." Slightly incongruous note to all this is added by such signs as POSTCARDS over a doorway, and THIS WAY OUT in lots of places and a very brightly lit red telephone box just behind the sentry's box and next to a cannon at the Byward Tower. When the detail has passed through the gate you are whisked in after them to watch the final phase. Several unorthodox military manœuvres perfectly timed so that just before the striking of ten and the blowing of a very feeling Last Post the warden pronounces " God Preserve King George." Sentries and detail reply "Amen." See how perfectly it is timed for yourself. The whole procedure takes approximately seven minutes, and has been going on for centuries. On your way out look at the Pool, seen between plane trees, lighted ships and the black sparkling water. Apply to the Resident Governor in writing stating date and alternative, and the number you wish to bring with you.

before going to bed

There are certain clubs (and we don't mean night clubs) which are designed to make the overseas visitor feel at home. (Amongst these are the English Speaking Union, 37, Charles Street, W.1, and the Over-Seas League, Over-Seas House, St. James's, S.W.1). Typical arrangements made are those of the Allies Club.

ALLIES CLUB, 6, Hamilton Place, W.1 (GROsvenor 4994). Started 1942 with the help of the Foreign Office. Many of the early members were refugees from Hitler and (in deference to them) no Germans are permitted to join; all other nationalities are accepted as members and it is a non-political club, for both men and women. There are two lounges, library, cardroom, two double bedrooms and eight single bedrooms. Restaurant serves a 5s. 6d. lunch and 6s. dinner, or à la carte, and the club is fully licensed. Natives have to be proposed by a member in the usual way (£6 6s. 0d. for men and £5 5s. 0d. for women) but if they live in the country they can join for the short periods they are in London (10s. 6d. a week). The club is mentioned because of its rules for overseas visitors; they can be recommended by their embassy or legation instead of by members (£1 a month). Bedrooms are 15s. 6d. a night, which includes bath and breakfast. President: Lord de la Warr. Secretary: W. J. Cude.

11 pm
NIGHT-CLUB TIME

It may help a little if we subdivide the places of night resort into three distinct categories, beginning with:

(A) *Restaurants*. Some do and some do not stay open into the small hours but either way they are open to all comers. It is simply a matter of you pays your money and you takes your choice. " Cheque-book " implies that your wallet will have to be tightly wadded.

(B) *Night-clubs*. These differ from restaurants in that only members and their guests are allowed right of entry. Membership may vary from ten shillings to ten guineas per annum. Normally it is necessary to wait for forty-eight hours (as a minimum) after filling in a form of application for membership, before being able to use the Club in question. Night-clubs differ from group C because they have different opening hours, generally 10.0 p.m. to 4.0 a.m. At almost all of them evening dress is optional and dark suit perfectly in order.

(C) *Clubs*. These are *not* to be confused with the old-established type of Pall Mall Club from whose windows purple old gentlemen stare fiercely into the street. They are poles apart. What we are dealing with here is a hybrid creature; and in its infancy at that. These Clubs are virtually restaurants where one can have luncheon, dinner, supper and also dance but—since they are Clubs— they are obviously only open to members and their guests. They do *not* come into the Night-club category because (i) they are open during the daytime, and (ii) they close down usually round about midnight or 1.0 a.m.

In many cases temporary honorary membership of both Clubs and Night-clubs is being considered by their managements. This means that the visitor will be able to join in an honorary capacity at a purely nominal figure (in some cases free of any entrance or subscription) but will yet enjoy the status and privileges of a full member. Best thing to do if you want to join is to go straight in, whatever time of the night, and ask the management what the procedure is. They will be only too glad to help you, so don't be nervous.

ALLEGRO (A)* 16, Bury Street, S.W.1 WHI : 6767	*Hours :* 6.0-2.30. *Dancing from 9.30.* *Theatre Dinner :* 12s. 6d. *Dinner and* *Dance :* 23s. 6d. *Cabaret. Two Bands :* *Swing and Rumba. Also : Ann de Nys* *at the piano.* 7.30-9.30. *Evening dress* *or dark suit.*	Unusual décor ; excellent food and service and, usually, pleasant people. Drinks are by no means inexpensive. For the early-birds, Ann de Nys at the piano, is *well* worth hearing.
LES AMBASSADEURS (B) & (C) 5, Hamilton Place, W.1 GRO : 6555	*Hours :* 12 noon-4 a.m. *Subscription :* 7 gns. *Entrance :* 5 gns. *Two bands,* *Paul Adam and Esteban.*	A night-club to beat all night-clubs, within the already powerful monolithic marble frame-work of the ex-Rothschild house. Apart from the lush orgiastic richness of the " Milroy " first floor late-nightery with its pendulous silk and disappearing ceilings, a large terraced garden overlooks Hyde Park—provides space for fine-weather revelry, and serves as roof for the private cinema below. In the ground floor bar and restaurant the Rothschild splendour still manages to shine through the lush new décor, and the magnificent staircase remains untouched. Other amenities : showers, a barber's shop, a travel agency, and—that essential—a library of the world's telephone books. Also a powder room which, in the words of the 6 ft. 4 in. 240 lb. proprietor, John Mills, is " no mere lavatory."
ASTOR (B) Fitzmaurice Place, Berkeley Square, W.1 GRO : 3181	*Subscription: Half a guinea. Entrance:* £1 *per visit. Hours* 9.0-4.0. *Two* *Bands. Cabaret.*	Specializes in first-class cabaret. Improved a great deal since it moved from its original home in Park Lane to Berkeley Square. Extremely popular, and justifiably so.
BAGATELLE (A) 1, Mayfair Place, W.1 GRO : 1268	*Hours :* 8.30-2.30 (*Sats.* 8.30-12.30). *Dinner and Dance :* 30s. *Two cabaret* *performances. Two Bands : Edmundo* *Ros and Arnold Baily. Evening dress* *optional. Manager : Arthur Brent.*	Very central. Excellent cuisine and prices to correspond. Formerly run by Ferraro after leaving the Berkeley and May Fair. Cheque-book.

* *The letter in brackets after the name gives you its category, as explained on the facing page.*

BERKELEY (A) 77, Piccadilly, W.1 REG : 8282	*Hours : 6.30-2.30. Dinner and Dance : 25s. Cabaret. Two Bands. Evening dress.*	Now coming back into its old form after a rather un-smart post-war patch. At its best the Berkeley can be unique.
CAFÉ DE PARIS (A) 3, Coventry Street, W.1 GER : 2036	*Hours : 8.30-2.30. Dinner and Dance : 30s. Cabaret. Two Bands. Evening dress except in balcony, where you can wear a dark suit.*	Perhaps not quite up to its unbeatable pre-war standard, nevertheless very good and pretty cosmopolitan. Specializes in good cabaret. Worth noting that upstairs you can eat very well and comparatively reasonably (at 25s.) and see the cabaret from the balcony but *not* dance.
CHURCHILL'S (B) 160, New Bond Street, W.1 MAY : 2635	*Subscription : 3 gns. Entrance : £1. Hours : 9.0-4.0. Two Bands. Cabaret.*	As popular as its namesake. The dim lighting does not prevent one from appreciating the new décor. Stag parties may not have much difficulty in finding dancing-partners who will help to while away the time.
CIRO'S (B) 39, Orange Street, W.C.2 WHI : 6966	*Hours : 12.30-2.30. Dinner and Dance : 35s. Two Bands (Ambrose & His Music and Samba.) Cabaret and Floor Show. Evening dress. Free " temporary honorary membership " for Overseas Visitors. Three months. Normal Conditions. Subscription : 10 gns. p.a., 5 gns. entrance.*	Has always been " in the money." Mink, sable, and diamonds in profusion ; and your bill to match. Very lush, very elegant and, largely due to Ambrose, not a little of its pre-war Ruritanian atmosphere. Cheque-book.
COCOANUT GROVE (B) 177, Regent Street, W.1 REG : 7675 (Night calls : REG : 6897)	*Subscription : 10s. 6d. Entrance : £1. Hours : 10.30-4.0. Cabaret. Two Bands.*	One of the old steady night-haunts of London. Just the place to visit after a regimental dinner, or for a not-too-tired business executive to go on to, after dinner, with his secretary ? Lots of fun.
COLONY (A) Berkeley Square, W.1 MAY : 1657	*(in conjunction with the Astor). Hours: 8.30-1.0. Dinner and Dance: 25s. 6d. Cabaret. Two Bands : Felix King and Santiago. Evening dress optional.*	Run in conjunction with its own night-club the ASTOR. (One has only to walk upstairs from one to the other.) This is NOT a Club—whereas the Astor is. Very good food and popular, especially with foreigners. Usually excellent cabaret.
DORCHESTER (A) Park Lane, W.1 MAY : 8888	*Hours : 6.0-2.30. Theatre Dinner : 12s. 6d. Dinner and Dance : One guinea. No cabaret. Two Bands. Evening dress.*	Has altered very little. Still very lush. If there are any millionaires, sterling, not dollar, they may be found here. Paradoxically, this does NOT mean that it is exorbitant—unless you intend to stay for a week.
EMBASSY (B) 6, Old Bond Street, W.1 REG : 5275	*Hours : 12.30-4.30. Subscription : 5 gns. p.a. Entrance (per member and guest) : 1 guinea. No cover charge. (i.e. à la carte). Cabaret. Two Bands.*	One of the oldest established clubs of its type in London, although possibly its former top-drawer character has changed somewhat with the passing of the years. Food and service excellent and usually a very high standard of cabaret. Cheque-book.

EMPRESS CLUB (C) 35, Dover Street, W.1 REG: 8100	*Hours* : 12 *mid-day-*4.30 *a.m. Subscription* : (*a*) *Dining-Dancing* : 5 *gns. Entrance* : 5 *gns.* (*b*) *Residential* (70 *Bedrooms*). 15 *gns. Entrance* : 5 *gns.* (*c*) *Business* (*i.e. for firms*) *on application.*	This place has a lot to offer, for, on the old-established residential side you may well meet elderly dowagers sipping " hock and seltzer " whilst in an adjoining room a rumba band is hotting up the guests. There is nothing like it in London; entertainment for all vintages. Excellent food and wine, and, of course you will need your cheque-book.
FOUR HUNDRED (B) 28, Leicester Square, W.2 WHI: 1813	*Hours* : 10.0-4.0. *Subscription* : 5 *gns. Entrance* : £1 *per member and guest. Tim Clayton and His Band. No Cabaret. Evening Dress.*	Still London's most exclusive night club. It is small, dark, hot, and usually packed out. Members go there to see, and be seen by, their friends. Manager, Rossi, is an autocrat and vets all applications for membership personally. Food adequate. Drink at bottle-party prices. Despite overcrowding and ensuing discomfort, it has " atmosphere " and is still the *only* place in London night life which retains any form of snob value.
GARGOYLE (C) 69, Dean Street, W.1 GER: 6455	*Hours* : *Bar*, 5.30-11.0 ; *Lunch*, 12.0-3.30 ; *Dinner*, 7.0-12.0 ; *closed Sundays. ALC menu. No cover charge. Average 12s. 6d. Evening dress optional. Subscription* : 1 *guinea. No entrance fee. Small band. No cabaret.*	Old-established haunt of the acting-writing-painting intelligentsia. At Soho rooftop level, private lift to fourth floor. Small pink room, with piano in the Tudor fire-place, gilt gargoyles. Down one flight into a Babylonian glass, mirror, gilt and brass, pink and gold world ; ample dance floor.
HATCHETTS (A) 1, Dover Street, W.1 REG: 1809	*Hours* : 6.30-2.30 (12.30 *Saturdays*). *Theatre Dinner* : 9s. 6d. *Dinner and Dance* : 17s. 6d. *Two Bands. No Cabaret.*	Not too formal and certainly *has* its individual atmosphere, which inclines towards heartiness. Patronized largely by the younger Naval officers. Has a lot to recommend it and is NOT expensive. Excellent dance music and good food.
JACARANDA (B) Walton House, Walton Street, S.W.3 KEN: 6865	*Hours* : 6.0-1.0. *Subscription* : 2 *gns. p.a. No entrance charge. Dinner and Dance* : 16s. 6d. *Bob Bisetto's Swing Quartet. No Cabaret. Dress* : *Dinner jacket or dark suit.*	Altogether excellent and moreover reasonable. Has been called ' the poor man's Four Hundred.' Was started by three ex-officers. Hand-picked, courteous and efficient staff. Food good but not sensational. By judicious vetting of applicants for membership the proprietors have, for the most part, managed to keep the place generally ' clean and tidy.' Only drawback, somewhat inaccessible from West End. One of the best small quiet bands in London.
LORELEI (B) 196, Grosvenor Road, S.W.1 VIC: 3386	*Hours* : 10.0-4.0. *Subscription* : 2 *gns. Entrance* : 10s. *per member and guest. No Cabaret.*	At the time of going to press this night-club has not yet opened ; but, as it is owned by the proprietors of the JACARANDA it is bound to be a success. It will be the only night-club, of its kind, overlooking the Thames and with an enchanting setting.
MAY FAIR (A) Berkeley Street, W.1 MAY: 7777	*Hours* : 8.0-*midnight. Dinner and Dance* : 17s. 6d. 6.0 *onwards. Theatre Dinner* : 12s. 6d. *No Cabaret. Band. Evening dress optional.*	Overseas visitors will be certain to run into some of their friends here. The atmosphere is not unlike that of Grosvenor House. Prices reasonable ; food and service good.

ORCHID ROOM (B) 28, Brook Street, W.1 MAY: 1212	*Subscription : 3 guineas. Entrance:* *15s. per member, 1 guinea per guest.* *Hours : 10.30-4.0. No Cabaret.*	Extremely popular and fashionable with the 'young things' ... who can afford it. Adequate food ; considerable cacophony. When a débutante says: " Let's go on to ..." this is where she wants to go. You can end up with eggs and bacon and the morning newspapers ... and Alka-Seltzers.
PHEASANTRY (C) 152, King's Road, S.W.3 FLA : 5326	*Hours :* 6.0-11.30. *Subscription :* *2 gns. p.a. No entrance fee. Dancing* *to radiogram. No Band. Dinner :* *8s. 6d.*	In the heart of Chelsea, so often and so wrongly called London's 'Mont-martre '—for nothing could be less like the very English Bohemia in and around the King's Road. René, the proprietor, opened the Pheasantry here in the heart of Chelsea long before the last war. The food is very good and the price reasonable. Dancing is incidental and only a secondary consideration. One visits the Pheasantry for a change from the West End, and to see what one can see. Remember the line: " What funny things you see when you haven't got your gun." ?
96 PICCADILLY (A) W.1 MAY : 9661	*Hours : Restaurant 9.0-1.30, Grill 6.0-* *midnight. Dinner and Dance : 25s. 6d.* *Cabaret. Two Bands. Manager : Egon* *Ronay. Evening dress optional ; but* *dark suit—and afternoon dress for* *ladies.*	When it opened, was patronized by H.R.H. Princess Margaret and accord-ingly became very popular. The food is good, and the service excellent. Be-cause it is on the small side one may be sure of individual attention and every-thing being done for one's comfort.
QUAGLINOS (A) 16, Bury Street, S.W.1 WHI : 6767	*Hours : 6.30-1.30. Dinner and Dance :* *23s. 6d. Three Bands. Jiving and Tzi-* *gane Cabaret. Manager : Louis Mol-* *ler. Evening dress optional.*	Still retains some of its pre-war cosy, *intime* atmosphere. Food, wine and ser-vice all first-class ; but not everyone likes fifty-fifty Gipsy music with their " swing."
RITZ (A) Piccadilly, W.1 REG : 8181	*Hours : 7.30-10.30. Dinner : 17s. 6d.* *No Cabaret. No Bands. Evening dress* *optional.*	One can't dance ; there's no cabaret (there was before the War), yet the food, the service, the setting and, for some inexplicable reason the people, are alto-gether admirable. But don't expect, as a newcomer, to find " Welcome " on the mat ...
SAVOY (A) Strand, W.C.2 TEM : 4343	*Hours : 7.30-2.0. Dinner and Dance :* *25s. 6d. Cabaret. Two Bands. Evening* *dress.*	Still extremely popular and good. Not unlike its pre-war self with excellent cabaret and good service. More the place for a party of six or eight than for those who wish to dine and dance *à deux.*
STORK ROOM (B) (Empress Club) 15, Berkeley Street, W.1 REG : 8100	*Hours : 11.0-4.0., 9.0-4.0 (Sundays).* *Entrance : £1. Two Bands. And* *'Al Burnett.' Dress Optional.*	This is probably the *only* night-club open on Sundays. It is a fledgling of the Empress Club. You are unlikely to have a dull moment here under the aegis of Al Burnett, who used to keep one amused at the Nut House not so long ago. An excellent host ; but you need hollow legs.
21 ROOM CLUB (B) 8, Chesterfield Gar-dens, W.1 GRO : 1710	*Hours : 7.0-2.30 Subscription: 5 gns.* *Entrance: 5 gns. Two bands, Delmundo* *and Henry Ziesel.*	Lush, soft-lit, self-conscious Edwardianism of plush and candelabrae. "Rico" Dajou, the temperamental host. The food is of a high order. A spasmodic cabaret is compensated by the extremely pleasant dining garden (in the sum-mer). But the club does not guarantee the weather.

12 midnight
on the Festival
NIGHT THOUGHTS

This seems to be the right moment, as you sip your Krug in the darkest corner of your chosen night-club, and before the cabaret comes on at 1.30, to tell your dancing partner about the South Bank Exhibition (remember you walked away from it at 12.0 noon)—after all, you've got to talk about something. Here is what we tell YOU. First thing, don't be misled by this talk of Edwardian, Victorian, pseudish, into thinking we dislike the modern movement (we practically invented it). Don't be misled, because we don't mention the Exhibition up till now, into thinking we loathe it. It means much to us. *Because* it is the first full-size example of modern architecture doing a popular job (an exhibition). *Because* it is doing that job for the man-in-the-street, not the æsthete in his ivory tower, or the financier behind his high wall. *Because* (pay attention please) for the very first time in history it is trying to create a still greater thing than architecture, a modern *background*, a 20th-century urban environment. For this deliberate effort to create urban environment, *The Architectural Review* has coined the word *townscape*—urban equivalent of landscape—the 18th-century landowner's deliberate effort to create a country environment.

TOWNSCAPE

And we really want to emphasize that this conception of *townscape* is worth getting hold of because it will put a new edge on your enjoyment of the Festival, and, come to that, of London. Take our advice and enter at the Chicheley St. Gate, thinking hard of townscape. The first thing you will notice is that the genius at work here, Hugh Casson, Chief Architect to the Exhibition, has ignored all the orthodox exhibition rules of Grand Avenue, Triumphal Way pimpled with fountains, leading up to the largest building; or a PLACE from which radiate the other main avenues. Instead he has put his biggest building (the Dome of Discovery) in one pocket and the Concert Hall in another, and has woven round them a subtle symphony of open and closed spaces through which, as you walk, you get a constantly changing series of vistas and a tremendous feeling of variety and size. As a matter of fact there *is* (for ease of circulation) a sort of central way through, but it's played down so hard you hardly know it's there. Instead you *weave*, coming here upon an oblique shot of a something from Mars, and then, suddenly, upon a full, a really tremendous *coup d'œil* of the Houses of Parliament across the river. Walter-Scott Gothic these, and you might suppose awkward customers to come up against in a slap-up 20th-century environment. Quite the contrary. See if you don't agree with us; *they never looked better*. And the same goes for the romantic but, by orthodox standards, hideous monster, Whitehall Court, which has been deliberately used by Hugh Casson to close the far end of his main square. This achieves not only a highly stimulating exchange of architectures, but effects of size and space which are simply staggering. For Whitehall Court is half a mile away across the Thames, not in the Exhibition at all. And yet, by hiding the Thames at this point, Casson makes it seem to be part of the Exhibition—the building that closes one end of his square—with more than Red-Square-Moscow effects of scale. To such good effect does he use the views of the historic buildings on the North Bank that one comes away feeling one has never seen them properly before.

It is amazing that by juggling now with this motif, now with that, by hiding the river, and then revealing it, by using levels, fly-over bridges, ramps and so on to alter the viewpoint of the visitor according to his height from the ground, Casson gets a variety of interest which makes the exhibition seem six times the size it is. Best example of changing levels, the Sea and Ships Pavilion on the river front which is not really a building at all, but a collection of large-scale exhibits:—ships' propellers, marine-engine, arranged on staging at various levels with gangways, cantilevers, ramps, so that the public can circulate amongst them. All the time you are stimulated by new vistas and feel life is good. Get the idea? St. Paul's against the latest thing in ferro-concrete. New and old as visual foils. Though modern themselves, the exhibition buildings have welcome on the mat for the north bank Old Faithfuls. Exactly what we hope will happen when the time comes to develop this site permanently (it was blitzed). This is townscape.

Here are a few of the things you mustn't miss:

ON THE RIVER BANK: the Skylon. You couldn't miss this anyway, because it is visible from most of the West End, a 290 ft. aluminium pencil supported on nothing and illuminated at night. Twentieth-century equivalent of the Eiffel Tower that adorned the Paris Exhibition of 1889.

The sculptured lion that used to adorn the Lion Brewery alongside Hungerford Bridge (demolished to make way for the concert hall) and re-erected in York Road at the foot of Waterloo Station approach, to mark the concert hall booking office. Made of *Coade Stone*, the mysterious synthetic material out of which so many of London's architectural enrichments were carved about the end of the eighteenth century. Interesting because the secret of Coade Stone has now been lost, and no scientist has succeeded in rediscovering it. An example of what might happen in a bigger way to a technocracy.

The corner in the LION AND UNICORN pavilion devoted to crazy inventions and other illustrations of the Englishman's congenital eccentricity.

In the COUNTRYSIDE PAVILION, an immense plaster tree on the branches of which are perched one stuffed specimen of every kind of bird that inhabits the British Isles.

In the POWER AND PRODUCTION pavilion the largest sheet of polished plate glass ever made—50 ft. long and 8 ft. 0 in. high.

The TELEKINEMA, where as well as television programmes the latest types of cinema film are shown, including stereoscopic films in colour and multi-stereophonic films in which the noises appear to come from all parts of the auditorium, as though the audience was in among the action depicted.

THE ROYAL FESTIVAL HALL, London's new permanent music centre with an auditorium seating 3,000, situated within a few yards of a railway bridge across which trains rattle and roar every few minutes, but thanks to the wonders of building science are quite inaudible within.

The old SHOT TOWER (temporarily a radar mast) in which shot was manufactured by the traditional method of dropping molten lead from a height into a basin of water until a couple of years ago. Magnificent interior views looking up. Don't miss this.

If you're INTERESTED IN HOUSING, it's worth a trip to Poplar in the East End to look at a model residential neighbourhood now under construction in an area flattened by bombing. It's called Lansbury and has been chosen as the " live architecture " exhibit of the Festival. It contains houses, flats, old people's homes, schools, churches, shops and a market square, and attached to it is the Festival's own temporary exhibition on town-planning and building sciences. Visit the " crazy house," designed to show the unfortunate results of all the mistakes that are made by unscientific builders. You can't miss the way to Lansbury: straight down Commercial Road and West India Dock Road, and when you get near you will see a giant decorated crane marking the spot. Notice by the way the street names in this traditional dockers' neighbourhood—Pekin Street and the like—a reminder of the flourishing days of the China trade.

At *Battersea Park*, James Gardiner, John Piper, Osbert Lancaster (illustrator of this guide) and many others have done things that will surprise you too.

1 am
CITY WALK

Don't get the idea from what's gone before that townscape is just another exhibition game. Far from it. Now that the moon is up and the traffic thinning out, what about an exercise in the real thing? Easier to concentrate when one can stand in the roadway without wounding the feelings of a bus driver. But what roadway? In this full moon? The City? The City of course.

CITY DESERTED

The City settles down to peace at an unbelievably early hour, not long after six. At 1.0 a.m. barring the odd bus and newspaper van, it's as though nothing had stirred in that jungle for a hundred years. A walk through the City in the full moon is a thing no one forgets. But if you prefer, the same walk can be done in daylight (with rather less chance of staying alive till the end).

Bow

Start at the altar steps of Bow Church from which, through West Window and door, can be seen, unbelievably beautiful in the full moon the dome and east end of St. Paul's. There isn't another view in London to compare with this product of the blitz. Buildings hid it before and buildings will hide it again unless, which is highly unlikely, the City decides to keep some open space where it would have a purpose, instead of keeping it for road traffic, where it hasn't. So see it while you may. Bow's own interior, roofless and fire-marbled, is that rare thing, a piece of pure architecture; but you may find the door locked—the British, like the Dutch, always lock everything they can—in which case your walk will have to start from the steps of the west door. Same view. Don't overlook, as you stand there, the weird effects (purely fortuitous, result of the blitz,) of the waste land round the Cathedral suggesting cliff and sea-scape, out of which rise single church towers and strange ruins, tantalizingly beautiful in the moonlight.

Garlickhithe

Now, make your way across Watling Street, down Garlick Hill, where (mornings) blue-chinned skinners and furriers, speaking all the languages under the sun, except English, do business on the street—and what a street—and with a thought, as you pass the door of St. James' Garlickhithe, for Jimmy Garlick in his glass case inside, pull up on the river bank at Queenhithe. Go down the river stairs and get your first real look at the river lights. The bridges west of you will be Blackfriars, road and rail.

water front

Now comes a great hooting of steamers (which means the tide is high), a strange homeless sound in the deserted dark street, and then the booming chime of Cathedral clocks, the two sounds which tell one sharper than words that one is on the water-front of the world's port. Authentic London. Turn East and you are confronted with a different sort of townscape, the great bulk of Cannon Street Station, typical product of that great Romantic utilitarian, the Victorian engineer. Enormous in size, prodigious in scale, reeking not of land's edge nor water's beginning, this half Crystal Palace thrusts its great bulk out over the river, presenting a mouth like a Zeppelin hangar to the little trains that crawl (at this hour only spasmodically) in and out over the echoing iron bridge. Thames Street dives through the black hole underneath. Here, once and for all, can be settled that thorny question of change of scale, which worries many people when they foresee gigantic modern buildings dwarfing the little neighbourhoods they know and love. First, modern buildings needn't be gigantic. But if they are, here is the answer. The scale of Thames Street and Cannon Street Station is hopelessly incompatible, yet the combination produces just that drama of contrast which the townscaper is on the look out for. Far from murdering each other they set each other off. We are in the presence, in fact, of one of those accidents of *laissez-faire* which have made of London a genuine piece of picturesque landscape. Besides such visual drama as this, the boulevards of Paris, though immensely pompous, are very elementary stuff.

pedestrian network

Under this archway one gains London Bridge. It's worth getting on the bridge just to look back at Cannon Street Station (there is a pink brick corner building jutting out into the street immediately at the foot of the station, which, with the twist of the street, is worth a small fortune as a landscape motif). Beyond London Bridge you are in Billingsgate (we shall be coming back at 5.0 a.m.) and can climb to those lanes above and beyond the Monument (looking back at a good piece of *Sharawaggi*—St. Magnus steeple against the glass windows of a modern building—on the way). These lanes must be recorded just because they have been overlooked by the wideners and straighteners. To any but the connoisseur of urban landscape they are probably rather dim and rather dirty little alleyways—George Lane and the Alley to St. Mary-at-Hill, Lovat (late Love) Lane, St. Dunstan's Alley, Idol Lane. But to those who realize that these courts and alleyways are the hangover of the mediaeval city plan, representing the sensible pedestrian scale of the place, knocked silly by undirected motor traffic, they are highly significant. You go *under* London Bridge and then turn left up Fish Street Hill, right into Monument Street, left up Pudding Lane, right into George Lane, which runs into Botolph Alley (pitch black, very romantic), which runs into the lane by St. Mary-at-Hill, which comes out down steps with a twist through a white-washed archway (which turns out to be a Wren doorway) under the great clock and West front of St. Mary. Of such sober alleyways the pedestrian network of London could be rebuilt—livened here by a piazza, there, where it has to go underground, by a crypt or cloister of the sort that takes one from Westminster School yard (see 12.0 noon) through the Dark Cloister to the Abbey.

Now that you're here, take a little more exercise and go down Seething Lane to St. Olave's, Hart Street (sacred to the memory of diarist Pepys) to Crutched Friars and so into that archway, still darker than the one under Cannon Street Station, known as French Ordinary Court. This court is certainly unique as to odour—not of the nuisances committed by little dogs, or by little boys who have not been arch-trained, does it smell, but of essential oils. Effect: that of a cinema when the attendant has gone by with the scent spray. The warm darkness, pitch black until your eyes get accustomed to it, is like the cinema too, until one feels cobbles underfoot and sees at last a dim lamp and the exit to Fenchurch Street. Fenchurch Street Station's flank, though inferior to Cannon Street, makes another fine backcloth to Crutched Friars. Under this, one can turn right into Cooper's Row. Cooper's Row *is* London. Or, since so much is blitzed, shall we say *was* London. So was, or is, that part beyond the Tower and Tower Bridge (which you can reach easily from here) where you join up with the Greenwich Walk (8.0 a.m.). Down St. Katharine's Way to Wapping High Street and the *Prospect of Whitby*. An even better time this (except that you can't get into a pub) for seeing the dock landscape, since blitzed wildernesses and horrors of LCC flat-land give place to the *terribilita* of night amongst giant warehouses, only half obscuring the midnight movement of great ships. If you want the very quintessence of London, wait at the swing bridge (which is the street) by St. John's Church, Wapping, and hear and watch the big ships moving (it's high tide, remember) round you—lights, darkness, gleams of water, dock walls, early nineteenth-century architecture (architecturally, St. Katharine's Docks by Telford are the best things on the waterfront). However, all this is most improper in a " city " walk, since you are well outside London Wall. Back to the Tower, please, or (since it is locked) to Tower Pier, just west of the sentry (look out for an open iron postern and the Eagle Steamer notices), where we will leave you overlooking the moonlit Pool of London, guarded to the east by the twin Gothic towers of Tower Bridge, a magnificent dream of half a century ago. Across the river, acting as a backdrop to this scene, the modern wharves. And in between the river, stretching to left and right, the working space for watermen, rivermen, pilots, tugmen, bargemen, policemen, firemen, customs officers, river rats and dock rats and the temporary resting place for deep-sea sailors from every other port in the world.

2 am
OPEN ALL NIGHT

As you wander back through deserted streets you may be wondering where you can get some aspirins to cure that headache, or something to quieten a rumbling tummy. Few though they are, here and there about the town you will see the lighted doorway of a chemist (prescriptions only), a post office, a church or a restaurant. We have combed the town and this is what we have found.

HUNGRY after that walk through the city? Not a hundred yards away is the Avenue Café in Aldgate Avenue (a stone's throw from Aldgate Tube)—open all night. Not only that, but you will get a good steak, or eggs (things you will not get in many other places). Hope you're used to army language. Décor is traditional, green and cream, green glass table tops, green plastic shakers, vinegar and sauce on each table; boxing match and Coca Cola ads, radio and net curtains (clean too). The kitchen, or should we say stove, is in the corner of the room and contributes to the atmosphere. If you want to ring up your hotel to cancel breakfast in bed there is a coin telephone right at your elbow. At your other elbow a taxi driver or a sailor just off his ship and going home.

STILL HUNGRY? Get that taxi driver to take you to S. Cohen in Wentworth Street (he's probably been there before). You are probably his last fare for the night so take him in with you for a cup of tea (in thick mugs) and a fresh pretzel. That's Mrs. Cohen behind the counter. We fear the combination of glass, marble and American cloth table tops won't match up to last night's snowy white linen, but you will still have the company of your driver.

AT THE OTHER END of town is the Yellow House Hotel, 8, Bayswater Road, open up to 3 a.m. (even after that, but it is risky). Ask Una, with a cigarette behind her ear, or Ann, who is only 18, to bring you a plate of spaghetti (Milanese or Bolognese). The restaurant is in the basement, two rooms, both filled with tobacco smoke, and the patrons are of a very mixed variety, nearest thing to quartier Latin. Check table-cloths, green leatherette modernistic chairs, and rough cast cream walls provide the setting. The spaghetti (and they have many other items) will cost you 3s., a cup of coffee 9d. Mr. Mitchell is in charge of the restaurant, and Mr. Eddie Meadows in charge of the hotel.

LYONS' CORNER HOUSE in the Strand is open ALL night, but after midnight only on the second floor. Help Yourself Service, prices more than usual (night staff is so expensive), Chocolate 9d., coffee 7½d., tea 5½d. Friday the best night, 2 a.m. to 3 a.m. the best time, to see the crowd of what looks like half the total of London's night owls. Head waiter (something more than just that), confidante and mentor is Mr. Clarke. Curious crowd including sailors, sundry sleeping characters, negroes with glasses of lemonade, two straws, bearded artists. In the basement Gent's cloakroom the following remedies may be obtained automatically by the insertion of a coin in one comprehensive machine: soda mints, cascara tablets, stomach powders, septic pencil, formalin and mint, aspirin.

OTHER ALL NIGHT HAUNTS include Minerva Restaurant, Baker Street; Tea Room, Paddington Station; Tea Bar, Waterloo Station; Café Quaradeghini, Borough High Street. And the Junior Turf Club, so known to generations of young chaps-about-town, meaning the coffee stall outside Hyde Park Gate at Hyde Park Corner.

BOOTS, Piccadilly, W.1. Most central of the all night chemists, gets a lot of its glamour from being in the heart of showland. Otherwise exactly like any other. Open for prescriptions only. Row of metal chairs for queuers. Most counters draped with dust sheets.

POST OFFICE, Charing Cross Road. Open for certain classes of business but not the best place to post your midnight letter. You can always send a telegram from a phone box remember.

ST. MARTIN-IN-THE-FIELDS CHURCH, Trafalgar Square. Overlooking busy pigeoned Trafalgar Square. A refuge from neon lights and the traffic.

THE OXFORD STREET BOOK SHOP (297). If you can't get to sleep, go and buy yourself a book here, any time up to 2.0 in the morning. Also foreign newspapers.

at your convenience

At the Gents, Hyde Park Corner, to look after you at night is Donald Sutherland. Fittings by John Doulton of London and Paris, usual fees. And if you have no money apply to Donald who will let you in for nothing.

IF THIS ONE DOESN'T PLEASE YOU, others at: Charing Cross Road, Men and Women; Embankment Gardens and Leicester Square, Men and Women; Piccadilly Circus, Men; Trafalgar Square, Men and Women; Victoria Embankment (Westminster Bridge), Men and Women; majority of other conveniences open from 8 a.m. to 11 p.m. or 11.30 p.m. on week-days and from 9 a.m. until 11 p.m. on Sunday.

3 am

ESCAPE into London

For eighteen hours the town is a howling free-for-all; for about six (not just once a life-time but every single day of its life) it becomes one of those lost ruins of the jungle, deserted except for some burning trees and prowling wild life, to be discovered afresh each time one is wise enough to stay out of bed. Now that you've done the *City* and the moon is still up, here's your big chance, while the town's off-guard, to escape into *London* (a very different place); the inner London, the London you won't really see from the top of a bus or behind a very big lorry in a very small street. Return for a re-check by daylight if you like, but for the first break-in, the night assault every time; remembering that the object is not so much to catalogue a fact as to uncover a secret. What follows covers so much of the jungle that it reads rather like a catalogue, but in fact it carries you into some of its most personal and revealing (but of course central) backwaters You'll need a car. If you haven't brought your own, indulge in a hired one from Godfrey Davis Ltd. of 7, Eccleston Street, S.W.1, SLO.0022, who will allow you to drive one of theirs (a five-seater Morris Oxford at 30s. for the first thirty miles and 1s. a mile thereafter). International Car Hire Ltd., 5A, Bathurst Street, W.2. AMB.7010, has cars to suit all pockets and tastes (from 8 h.p. Morris at £1 a day plus 5d. a mile to a 18 h.p. Standard Vanguard at 30s. a day plus 9d. a mile, even chauffeur-driven Rolls Royces). If driving yourself, don't forget to take enough money for a deposit, £10 in this case. Remember not to blow your horn as it will disturb the night life of the jungle.

Belgravia

Get them to put you on your way to Eaton Square—the largest square in London, mainly Regency, porticoed, many-storied, basemented. At one time badly threatened due to requisitioning and consequent neglect. King's Road right down the centre (one time royal route from St. James's Palace to Hampton Court), this portion tree-lined and stately as before urbanization. Belgrave Street (left), passing St. Peter's, Eaton Square (for fashionable weddings), into Belgrave Square. And on the corner between Grosvenor Crescent and Wilton Crescent, at the end, the Ruritanian Embassy, location of film, " Fallen Idol," tall, stuccoed, evocative. This is Embassy-land anyway, and in the Square, beside a copious number of houses " TO LET " (houses such as these provided home comfort for Victorian families, but are now split into any number of flats), are the Spanish, Norwegian, Saudi Arabian and Mexican Embassies. Coast up Wilton Crescent, restored Georgian, then dive suddenly into Wilton Row and find yourself in a completely different world. Hence our word "escape." Mews, in fact, to Wilton Crescent, cobbled and sporadically pavemented and full of pink houses and bay trees which were once coachmen's quarters, now madly sought after and trying to live down its mews location. Near the end the " Grenadier " (see 6 p.m.), one of London's quiet and most secret pubs, entrance door up a flight of steps. Beside it, Old Barrack Yard with centre gutter beaconed by gas lamp and screened by a creepered trellis. Kinnerton Street (left) is really what we have been leading you to, supreme, the most cosy and romantic of all mews. A composite of London town life of the " hidden " type, two-storey houses with bright front doors up a couple of steps, potted trees carelessly left in the roadway, window boxes. The corner cobbler, knee boots and old leather trunks in the window, the dairy and public house side by side. On one side garages, above them flats, further along a giant plane tree, dominating. Although named Street, completely mews in character, a secluded backwater, with a pleasant twist. " The Horse and Groom," well worth a visit (not previously mentioned). In contrast, carry on to Belgrave Mews, through Motcomb Street (right) with made-to-measure shops, bright and glossy, eager to attract customers, and the Pantechnicon, yellow Doric-columned furniture repository. Left and left again into West Halkin Street, Belgrave Mews (right) with arched entrance, strait-laced but tremendously dramatic as seen between tall houses, cobbled roadway. " Star Tavern " this end and coachmen's flats, but with now very different type owners, who have an eye for colour, especially yellow, and tubbed evergreens.

Brompton

Out the other end, Pont Street (right), source of the phrase " Pont Street Dutch," through Beauchamp Place, a sudden outcrop of class shops, to Brompton Road (left), plebeian, tree and antique shop lined, fluorescently lit, into Cheval Place (right), so narrow that you will wonder how you ever got through, a forced turn to the right and then an obligatory one to the left. Now in Rutland Street and an area, for some strange reason, entirely overlooked by the spec. builder—to Montpelier Place (right, out of Montpelier Walk), charming, delicate two-storey houses with basements delightfully and slenderly railed. At the end the German Evangelical Church, ornate, weather-worn white stone like a cream cake amongst a lot of buns. Beautiful Montpelier Square (left), calm and unruffled by the two out-of-London arteries of traffic so close on either side. Trevor Place (right and left), leading to Kensington Road (left), stretching to Kensington, skirting Hyde Park and Kensington Gardens, tall unmanageable 19th-century houses, largely replaced by 20th-century flats of red brick and metal windows with underground garages. Detour down Ennismore Gardens (left), passing Romanesque All Saints Church, set well back, a ghostly reminder of Italy. Ennismore Gardens Mews, entered through a magnificent Corinthian-columned portal, out of this world; one-sided row of mews houses with wrought iron ornamental gates and window boxes, facing gardens. Back to Kensington Road by Princes Gardens (left), Exhibition Road (right). Albert Hall and Albert Memorial impossible to miss. Hyde Park Gate, in two parts (left), worth driving down (dead end), but a typical London street; every type of 19th-century architecture, quite a range of 20th-century inhabitants. Most popular, Winston Churchill, in neo-Georgian re-faced house at the far end (on right), with policemen outside sometimes. And on his right, No. 29, Lady Jones (novelist Enid Bagnold) who once solved her milk problem by urbanizing a cow. Opposite, gaunt Kensington Dutch creeper-covered house, No. 18, Epstein, you can see (if you don't mind gawping) some of his last, and possibly his well-known, models through the windows. Indians, Austrians, the nobility and ordinary folk fill the rest of the road. Note the two (Nos. 10 and 12) complementary stucco houses, nearly at the top of the street (on left), each flourishing a single bulky two-storey asymmetric Corinthian column by the front door. Other section of Hyde Park Gate is the hopeful, two-storey house-in-the-country type. Glance down Reston Place, charming courtyard.

Kensington
Palace Gate (left), note No. 10, a (1938) modern block by Wells Coates, in the best pre-war modern tradition. Leads to Victoria Grove (right), leafy street of small mid-19th century houses with delightful tin porches and wooden trellises, surprising in Kensington. (On the corner of Canning Place, similar in character to Victoria Grove, and De Vere Gardens is one of the few mews stables which still has horses—Hacks for Hire, on the first floor.) Into St. Alban's Grove, slightly larger houses, pleasant, Kensington Court Place (right) and Thackeray Street (left) into

Kensington Square, in the best Georgian tradition, (right) into Derry Street, between two monster modern department stores, large, stone-faced, fronting Kensington High Street (left), and Wrights Lane (left again), into Marloes Road and Scarsdale Villas (right), front-gardened. Cross into Pembroke Square, completely domestic, front-gardened, three-storey, late Georgian. Right at the end into charming Edwardes Square (very much sought after), passing the " Scarsdale," forecourt stacked with rustic seats ready for the rush of open-air loving patrons, Edwardes Square South (left) given over to artists' studios, (right) at the end, turn right again (before the end) to drive down the north side of the square, complete country lane effect, gravelled road, high-walled one side, trees and gardens the other (three lefts and a right) into private road, late Georgian row (fronted by semi-private, tree-lined lawn), a grand façade for Kensington High Street. Melbury Road (right, right and left), road of homes of the great Victorians, Holman Hunt, Leighton, Watts, very typical of its day, note large north light windows. Addison Road (right), spacious, not much used (look out for faïence-fronted home of Halsey Ricardo).

Notting Hill
Leads to Regency Royal Crescent, worth driving round, Tuscan-columned porticos, Holland Park Avenue (left), houses with stock motifs which take on a surrealistic significance of strangeness (22, 24 to 28, 25, 62). Norland Square (on left), Campden Hill Square (right), exciting contours here, another worth while detour, back across to Ladbroke Grove, full of trees, to Ladbroke Square (right), across the communal (but private) gardens which are the great town planning feature of this part of London and make it one of the best to live in (houses are planned with their backs to a park), Ladbroke Terrace (right) and at the bottom some of the nicest Regency cottages you could ever find. Campden Hill (across and left), waterworks dominating, and " Windsor

Castle " at the top. Holland Street (left), 1840 houses with poplar-guarded cul-de-sac, charmingly rural. If before midnight, turn (right) into Kensington Church Street and Kensington High Street (left) and Kensington Palace Gardens (left). This is tree-lined, rustic-fenced, joining Notting Hill Gate to High Street, Kensington. Strictly private, except to residents and their visitors. Guarded by a beadle and closed at night. Begun 1843: the early conception of a street of Palaces. In fact, a millionaire's row designed by Barry, T. H. Wyatt, Owen Jones, Knowles, etc.; sufficiently detached from each other to allow discrepancy in styles of architecture to intermingle without clashing. Notice Baroda House, at the end, white, even the chimney pots show Indian influence. The street occupied by, amongst others, Soviet and Nepalese Embassies, two Legations, a Marquis, a Duchess, and a Cabinet Minister (if the Beadle stops you, say you are going to the Soviet Embassy). Bayswater Road (right) and Orme Square (left) (worth driving round), mixed styles, but quiet, unlike Bayswater, building of it financed by Ackermann.

Bayswater
Behind this grand Bayswater façade facing Hyde Park and stretching to Marble Arch, a district of small hotels and boarding houses (houses which nowadays do not permit a squadron of maids and cooks per family). Albion Street (left) and Albion Mews (right, entrance under houses) charming, dead-ended by modern block of flats, but partly sided by Tyburn Burial Ground (which is what it sounds like—the burial place of felons hung at Tyburn, scaffold marked by triangular stone set in roadway at Marble Arch), now the chief playing field of Toxophilite Society. If not that energetic, turn off at Leinster Terrace (left), left-hand side still remains two-storey village street. Leinster Gardens, 23 and 24, remarkable as dummy fronts hiding a cutting of underground railway. Porchester Terrace (left and right at end) with a glimpse, on right, of Paddington's vast new housing scheme; a ghost road, deserted and crumbling houses, windowless, barbed wired. On to Harrow Road (right), a typical Paddington " Blue Lamp " street. Westbourne Terrace Road (left) takes you across Regent's Canal to Blomfield Road (right), reminiscent of a Dutch canal scene with the stuccoed houses of the London of 1840, (the scarcely known Pearson church across the canal) and Browning's house (the poet's), derelict, climax the pool (called Browning's Pool) ended by bridge and lock-keeper's cottage, in fact is Paddington Basin (also known as Little Venice, new resident added " e " to his sign " Beware of the Dog ").

St. John's Wood
Now for the nightmare of Edgware Road (left), with Clifton Court, Stockbroker's Tudor style facing you. St. John's Wood Road (right), Hamilton Terrace (left), probably the widest residential street in London. Hall Road (right), Circus Road, melée of 20th-century flats and neo-Georgian country villas in own gardens, into St. John's Wood Terrace, single-storey shops built in front gardens to begin with (notice front gardens later on); a crumbling Corinthian-columned temple (once chapel), then squash court, and St. Marylebone Alms Houses (1836), small, two-storeyed, with 19th-century feeling still clinging to them; Towns-

hend Road (right) leading to Prince Albert Road (left), Park Lane residential flats taking advantage of view of Regent's Park and south sun. North Gate (left and right) will take you into the park and Outer Circle (left) past Zoo, listen for lions and don't leave the car. Gloucester Gate (left).

Camden Town
Albany Street (right) and charming Park Village West (left), stucco houses (completely out-of-town atmosphere) irregularly placed along a winding road, back gardens facing valley (once a canal). Back into Albany Street (left), barracks and warehouses, Cumberland Gate (right), and Outer Circle again (left), Regency terraces, film-set-like, cream painted, well preserved, magnificent in their unity. Chester Gate (left), Albany Street (right), Longford Street (left) leading into Drummond Street, brings you to

Euston Great Arch, one of the greatest pieces of architecture in London (1838 Doric-columned approach to Euston Station), which, of course, the railways are always trying to pull down.

Bloomsbury
Euston Grove (right), Euston Road (left), Woburn Place (right), and on the left, splendid, perfect model of the Erechtheum, St. Pancras Church, built by Inwood, 1819-22, one of the great pieces of neo-Greek architecture in London. Tavistock Place (left) leading to Regent Square, tidy for this part of London and tree-scaped, Georgian, intimate houses; one side blitzed revealing the most modern post-war council flats; neo-Greek Presbyterian Church at the end, built for Edward Irving, 1824-7, boarded up but intriguing.

Finsbury

Sidmouth Street, Ampton Street, King's Cross Road (left), stark East End industrial; Great Percy Street (right) passing through Percy Circus (slipping down the hillside and badly bombed) leads to Myddleton Square, Islington, made glamorous by Arnold Bennett in *Riceyman Steps*. Drive round it, out at River Street where square motif is carried on, into Lloyd Square, simple pediment motif again carried on, down Lloyd Baker Street, Calthorpe Street, to Gray's Inn Road (left) and Gray's Inn, on your right. Staple Inn in front of you, one of London's nicest secret places. Lincoln's Inn built to the dimensions of the plan of the Great Pyramid (which is four-sided), (right, into Holborn, then left). And the Middle Temple, the other side of Fleet Street, a chain of quiet private squares devoted to the Law, from which we would take you (north-westwards) to Bedford Square (finest of London's squares, built about 1770, notice the doorways) designed all-in-one and still standing like that, and then south through St. Martin's Lane, still one of the most evocative of the West End's streets (and much more important before Charing Cross Road was driven through 80 years ago), chiefly because of the portico of St. Martin's that closes the vista. Notice (right) the Salisbury pub (see 6 p.m.) and Harrison's printing works (left), with which our escape into London may be allowed to end, since here, quite literally, is where it started, Harrison's being printers of this Guide. Kind of firm we like to think of as typical of London, founded in the 18th century by a Harrison and still run (and now one of the biggest printers) with immense verve by the Harrison clan whose work you know well since they print all the (British) stamps you stick on your letters (a hundred and twenty-four million a week, seven thousand million a year). However, the front of the building is the picture we want you to end up with, evoking as it does, even to the Royal Arms over the door, the very distillation of the London of Cruikshank, Dickens, Thackeray, Leach—the London into which we would all so thankfully escape.

4 am

TURKISH DELIGHT

Too late to go home now with markets coming on at 5.0, but just a little heavy in the head? As usual we have the solution, for the gentlemen anyway. The Savoy Turkish Baths, 92, Jermyn Street, W.1, will solve all your troubles (once under the steam you lose the fight in you). Open

24 hours a day, 7 days a week, you can go at any time (naturally) and for the charge of 10s. 6d. (at night 8.0 to 8.0, by day it is only 6s.) you can have your Turkish Bath and then sleep it off in a private cubicle, where you can stay until 12.0 if you came in late (or should we say early). The usual time to leave is 10 a.m. having had your breakfast for an additional 3s. 6d., roughly. Never too full. A. L. Pegg in charge. Three hours will give you the full benefit of the treatment, but, sorry, you've only got one right now. Ladies less fortunate. They will have to get their drinking done early; no admission after 6.0, or before 8.0. Their baths at 12, Duke of York Street (WHitehall 7125). The cost for the basic is 7s. 6d. and you can get a list of the extras from them. Refreshments. Miss Porter at the head of the fully trained staff. No waiting list, always ready to oblige. For the men again, we have an alternative. We recommend the Imperial Hotel, Russell Square, W.C.1; the baths are in the sub-sub-basement—decayed Edwardian atmosphere—Turkey carpets—the remains of expensive oriental décor. The ruthless attendant will rub you down just as vigorously here as elsewhere. (Tell him when he does so to add half-a-crown, to the bill, for himself.)

5 am
FISH

On the approach to London Bridge you have a grandstand view of London's roughest, toughest, market. Not your first view of Billingsgate (we were there at 2 a.m.), but what a difference. Could this be the same city? Below you, Lower Thames Street, lorries and carts stacked with crates of fish, an unforgettable smell. Go down the gas-lit steps (buy morning paper on the way).

IN AMONGST IT

And now LOOK OUT. There's no room for you, and no time for you. Mind the cracked ice and the white coated, leather hatted (known as billy-cocks, direct descendants, so it is said, of bowmen's helmets worn at Agincourt) porters. Fight your way to the hall and see the fish under brilliant light. If you have not had enough close shaves, have a haircut, any time after seven, at the Coal Exchange Barber Shop opposite the hall. Climb up Love (Lovat) Lane (no longer moonlit) and perhaps at Brammer and Morck (No. 10) they will show you the tanks of live Danish eels in the basement. A little further up, turn left in Botolph Alley. Look for George's Snack Bar, where George himself will be filling the pans in the window with fat, ready for the day's fry of sausages and onions. Go in for a cup of tea, a cheese or bacon sandwich. Sit down at a marble-top table. Bright lights and embossed wallpaper to make you feel at home. Sooner or later a porter will come downstairs and hand George a key. He's been changing into working dress. Look out for the girl behind the gas stove. With the smell of fish strong in your nose you might like to remember that these smells have been floating around for a thousand years, although not exclusively, because, until William III's time the market also dealt in all kinds of provisions. Billingsgate Wharf, the oldest wharf on the river, was not only used by fishing boats, but also by small vessels, and what more convenient place for a market than at the wharfside? There's a rumour that the name derives from Belin, a king of the Britons. The building in which the market is now held was designed in 1877 by Sir Horace Jones (who also designed Smithfield Market and Tower Bridge).

6 am
AND CHIPS

And now for Borough Market. Cross over London Bridge, passing the first of the 100,000 (probably charladies) for the day. Another cup of tea? *Price's* red wagon at the south end, belching smoke like some misplaced caravan, will give you the hottest cup you ever drank. And before continuing, notice on your left and right, Nos. 1 and 2, London Bridge (survivors, in street numbering only, of the houses once crowding the bridge, alas, now long removed, this reminder of the old days). You are now in Borough High Street (and a bit further up are remains of the Marshalsea Prison).

Borough Market

And here on the right down a flight of steps (before the railway bridge) is the Borough Market, the poor man's fruit and vegetable market, distributing to south and south-east (the poorer areas of London). Here, in the shadow of Southwark Cathedral and under the arches that carry the trains to Cannon Street and Charing Cross (look up and see the pattern of the train lights on the glass roof), are crates of grapefruit from Jamaica, pears and onions from Holland, oranges from Spain, Canadian apples, Italian cauliflowers, Belgian grapes, tomatoes from the Canary Islands. But items depend on the season, so see what you can find. Look out for the gas lighting (there is still some), the old bollards, the beadles (they look like chauffeurs and are there to take a toll on everything that comes in). And if you are still full of fight there is a wonderful early morning stagger, down past Southwark Cathedral, through granite-setted alleys of flour mills and dark archways (look out for cranes) to the River, Barclay's Brewery (Dr. Johnson's Mrs. Thrale), the Anchor (see 6.0 p.m.), Clink Street, Bear Yard (bear-baiting) and Shakespeare's *Globe*. Back to Bankside in fact, with St. Paul's dome across the river aglitter in the rising sun.

Covent Garden

From here an early bus over Blackfriars Bridge will get you close to Covent Garden Market, one time Westminster Convent Garden, later a piazza, designed by Inigo Jones and a meeting place for market gardeners, later still a market—*the* market. Visit it between 5 and 8 a.m. Buy your vegetables or a bunch of flowers here. They start selling at 6.0; your vegetables at Solomon's and flowers, before 11.0, in the Flower Market. Have a cup of " char " from Mackay's van under the portico of St. Paul's, the actors' church (setting for the first act of Shaw's *Pygmalion*), or the Jem Café, open all night). See the foreign fruits within the glass Romanesque interior of the Floral Hall, popular as a promenade with patrons of the Royal Italian Opera House in 1860, which was designed by the same architect as the Hall (Barry). The Opera House is just beside you, and for a pub (open for the porters) there is *The Kemble's Head*.

other markets

London's other wholesale markets, all interesting in their way, are: SMITHFIELD, off the Farringdon road, one time fairground (Bartholomew Fair, resurrected by the Old Vic this season in Ben Jonson's play of that name). Execution ground. Dealt in live cattle till 1861. Not much action here with the present state of the meat ration. LEADENHALL, charming street intersection, roofed with glass and lined with poultry and fish wholesalers. Lit by gas. Roman forum of old City of London. SPITALFIELDS, vegetable wholesale market for the East End. The Spitalfields area was once largely occupied by silk-weavers, partly descended from Huguenot refugees.

OPEN ON SUNDAY

There is a strange tradition that a London Sunday is dull. It is—for the dull. For those who don't find music "dull", it offers top-grade singing, organ music, afternoon concerts; for those who are not dulled by religion, a panorama of great rituals and services for Protestants, Catholics, and of course all the others; for those who prefer "life" in the comparatively raw, a whole series of morning markets which are as bizarre as they are useful; for those who don't like "life" at all, the Sunday cinema, the owlish afternoon queue, or equally unreal morning goings-on in Hyde Park. Hyde Park was once, still is to some extent, a great Sunday Promenade (though no longer of the *bon ton*), with the Serpentine on one axis (boats, ducks, the lido), and on the other, Marble Arch with a special Sunday vintage of public speaking (see 9 p.m.), whose charm lies in its extremes—extremes of piety, of blasphemy.

STREET MARKETS

Sunday markets, the kingdom of coster, spiv and barrowboy, are held in certain set streets Sunday mornings. Most famous, Petticoat Lane, where you can get—well, anything. At least two more within spitting distance. They belong very specifically to the East End, and will give you good squalid fun and strange new sensations—scent of oranges and a whelk stall, blended with the aroma of an Aldgate Jew's cigar, all posted to you (so to speak) in an envelope of dance music coming in great warm gusts from the radio stall. Leave your wallet and knuckleduster behind, but not your girl, though she must be ready to be a sardine. Fantastic crowd scenes amid deserts of blitzed buildings.

THE BIG ONES are Petticoat Lane (Middlesex Street); Club Row (Brick Lane); Chapel Street (Islington, N.1); and on the South Bank, East Lane (Walworth, S.E.16). Columbia Road for potted plants (Columbia Road, Club Row, and Petticoat Lane are all within walking distance). There will be a few stalls in Lambeth Walk, but Soho will be deserted, and so will the New Cut.

WEEKDAYS, JUST THE REVERSE, with the big markets in the Cut, (Waterloo Road, S.E.1); Mile End Waste (Whitechapel, E.1);

Leather Lane (Holborn, E.C.1); Berwick Street (Soho, W.1); also, across the Thames, Lambeth Walk (Lambeth, S.E.1) and Brixton (Brixton Road, S.W.9). Perhaps the most lurid is Portobello Road (N. Kensington—"the Porto"). For a typical picture of the vicissitudes of a London street get off your bus at Notting Hill Gate and start walking down the " The Porto " from its source (but on a Friday or Saturday, not on Sunday).

SUNDAYS. Petticoat Lane is the King Pin. Favourite time 10.0-1.0. Here you can buy blue jeans, muffins, bread, wet fish and shell fish, atlases of Israel, motor-scooters, lino, a sideboard, an accordion, a camera, binoculars, a watch. And at East Lane, a vintage cauliflower ear belonging to the pugilist Tommy Noble who will also sell you his oils. If your week-end needs run to live turkeys, rabbits in a hutch, Alsatian pups, or even a nice goat, these can be acquired in Club Row (Brick Lane), by Bishopsgate Station, which is the great animal market. Also geese, ducks, broody hens, caraway seeds, canaries, bowls of goldfish, greyhounds and racing pigeons. Also, since the street-market shops are mostly open too, smoked salmon (Lupman, 100 Brick Lane), Torah mantles and praying hats (2s. 6d. to 4s), or a signboard done in Hebrew (Ritter, 86, Brick Lane). Also (and of course), oranges, from seedless to " blood ovals " (" Malta bloods— they're the sort—just off the new boat—good as a glasser-wine "). If, on the other hand, you happen to have locked your suitcase back at the hotel and lost the key, you may have to take a taxi to the market at Chapel Street, Islington, where at the far end from the Angel, on the right, sits a gentleman who will cut a new one while you wait. (Remember to take your suitcase with you too.) Useful sort of man. The crowd will consist of Hebrew race-gangs, cockneys in mufflers, spivs in belted coats, Aldgate jewesses, lascars, publicans, lodging-house keepers, policemen and a sprinkling of old-time costers.

MUSIC IN CHURCHES

On week-days, before the war, church organ recitals during the lunch hour were a feature of City life. Very few recitals are given nowadays, but the following are worth noting:

ORGAN RECITALS, once a week, in the lunch-hour, at *St. Michael's, Cornhill*, and at *St. Margaret's, Westminster*. Lunch-hour recitals, also every other Thursday, at *St. Paul's Cathedral* and at *Westminster Abbey*, during the Festival. In addition, special organ music will be played during the daily services at Westminster Abbey.

A FEW CHURCHES have recitals by instrumentalists or singers. Soloists every other Tuesday at *St. Martin-in-the-Fields*, at 1.10 p.m., and every Thursday at *St. Botolph's, Bishopsgate*, at 1.10 p.m. For further details of recitals, concerts and dramatic performances in churches, get in touch with the following church information centres:—the Festival Church St. John's, Waterloo; St. Anne's House, Dean Street, Soho; the YMCA and the YWCA, Great Russell Street, W.C.1; and St. Martin-in-the-Fields, Trafalgar Square.

SUNDAY SERVICES

This is not an age of great preachers or of first-class amateur music-making. But for many a service of worship cannot be wholly satisfying unless the music or preaching (or both) is of the highest standard. For such the following information is intended.

CHURCH OF ENGLAND. Westminster Abbey, most certainly first on the list. Standard of music in the services here is exceptionally high. Ceremony and ritual perfect. Adjoining the Abbey, *St. Margaret's*, mother church of Westminster and official church of the House of Commons, has a reputation for scholarly preaching. Outstanding intellectual sermons by Canon Charles Smyth. Distinguished also as preachers are Rev. P. N. Gilliat, vicar of Holy Trinity, Brompton Road (good music, crowded), and Canon F. H. Gillingham, the famous cricketer, at St. Michael's, Chester Square (also crowded). Most crowded of all perhaps (doors have to be locked at Easter) is *St. Martin-in-the-Fields* in Trafalgar Square, the church which the late Dick Sheppard made known as the " Parish Church of the Empire " during the 'twenties. In those days of great unemployment the church established a reputation for the social work carried out there. Still an important social centre. Tradition of social work and good popular preaching rather than of music. Excellent congregational singing.

St. Mary Woolnoth, Lombard Street, the evangelical centre in the City, where John Newton, the 18th-century hymn writer, preacher and reformer, carried out his most important social work. Another evangelical church, *St. Paul's*, Portman Square, notable in that its congregation does not expect the conventional twenty-minute address, but is frequently harangued by its preacher for anything between sixty and ninety minutes. Founder of world-famous Toc H is Tubby Clayton at All Hallows Berkynge Chirche by the Tower (assistant priest, Rev. G. Huelin).

For high musical standards, *All Saints'*, Margaret Street (Anglo-Catholic, a centre for churchmen in the West End), *St. Sepulchre's*, Holborn, and *St. Michael's*, Cornhill, are in a class by themselves.

Good music also at:—*St. Paul's Cathedral, Chapel Royal*, St. James's (enquire about admission), *Southwark Cathedral, St. Paul's*, Knightsbridge, *St. Peter's*, Eaton Square, and *St. John's*, Waterloo Road: St. John's, which has been rebuilt as the Festival Church after extensive damage by bombing, is being used during the Festival for daily services and for sacred concerts, religious plays, missionary addresses and lectures. Visitors will have the chance of hearing lunch-time addresses by leading preachers of all denominations from all over the country.

ROMAN CATHOLIC. Principal Roman Catholic churches in London include *Westminster Cathedral*, notable for its music, *Brompton Oratory* and the *Church of the Jesuit Fathers*, Farm Street, the great teaching church of the Jesuits.

CHURCH OF SCOTLAND. One of the outstanding preachers in London is Dr. Robert V. Scott, of *St. Columba's*, Pont Street. The church was damaged by bombing and services are now held in Jehangier Hall, the Imperial Institute, Exhibition Road, South Kensington. Always large congregation.

NON-CONFORMIST CHURCHES. Rarely notable for their music, but they make up for this by having the best known popular preachers. The Congregational denomination has the Rev. Leslie Weatherhead (famous for his " popular theology " books) of the *City Temple*. His church was destroyed during the war and services are now held at *Marylebone Parish Church*, Edgware Road, W.1. More evangelical type of ser-

mon at the other principal Congregational church, *Westminster Chapel*, Buckingham Gate. The Methodist church has two fine preachers in the Rev. W. E. Sangster, of the *Methodist Central Hall*, Westminster, and the Rev. Dr. Donald Soper, whose sermons are worth the price of sitting in the dreary *Kingsway Hall*, Holborn. The principal church of the Baptist denomination is *Bloomsbury Central Church*, Shaftesbury Avenue.

SALVATION ARMY. This resumé would not be complete without a reference to something peculiarly British—the Salvation Army. This large body of practical Christian socialists is as remarkable for its organizational ability as is the Roman Catholic Church. And the Army's General, in London, may be compared with the Pope, in that when he makes a statement that statement holds good for all his followers in every part of the world. Those who may feel inclined to scoff at the Salvation Army, with its military caps, poke bonnets, brass bands and embarrassingly sentimental hymns, should attend one of the evening services (Sundays, Wednesdays and

Fridays) at *Regent Hall*, Oxford Street. They will detect here the enthusiasm which gives the Army its strength and its discipline.

CHILDREN'S CHURCH. In the last twenty-five years visitors to London from all parts of the world have travelled the thirty-minute journey to see the Children's "Little Church," attached to *Ealing Green Congregational Church*, Ealing Green (near Ealing Broadway Station). Children's services are held in this miniature church every Sunday morning, while parents attend the service in the main church. The older children among the one hundred members have their own group of deacons which meets every week, under an adult chairman, to prepare for the next service. The scheme has proved to be more effective than the average Sunday school in keeping children in the Church as they grow up. The building is always open and visitors can be sure of a welcome from ex-R.A.F. padre, Rev. B. Railton Bax, who lives in the adjoining Manse.

FOR TIMES OF SERVICES see *The Times* on Saturday. During the Festival all the churches will combine every Sunday to hold a meeting in the open-air theatre at Battersea Park Festival Gardens.

index